SECOND SPRING PART VIII

I CONFESS TO YOU

E. M. Abear, BSc., M.D.

AuthorHouse™
1663 Liberty Drive
Bloomington, IN 47403
www.authorhouse.com
Phone: 833-262-8899

This book is printed on acid-free paper.

ISBN: 979-8-8230-0712-2 (sc)
        979-8-8230-0714-6 (hc)
        979-8-8230-0713-9 (e)

Print information available on the last page.

Published by AuthorHouse 05/05/2023

authorHOUSE®

DEDICATION

This book is heartily dedicated to my confessor,

Emeritus Rev. James Shurtleff
Notre Dame Church
Ogdensburg, New York 13669

&

To my loving wife,

Imelda R. Abear, MD., FAAP
Pediatric Medical
St. Laurence Psychiatric Hospital
Ogdensburg, New York 13660

PREFACE

"Childhood Foibles: growing-up in a large family" brings in childhood memories we want to forget yet still continues to remember because of the lessons gained as we go through life.

Part I of the book provides very interesting insights into the typical teenage behavior including harrowing experiences of a child as he moves-on towards adulthood. Honesty, sincerity and candidness mark the narration of events in this book and how such experiences made him realize the goodness of God and the evils of Satan.

Descriptions of his thoughts and actions that led him to do things for Satan are actually common among male children of his age fighting for their survival in a large Filipino family, living in a typical cultural environment during the World War II (mid- 1940s) period.

How the author, with his physical deviation causing his inferiority, survived the difficulties in life and the discriminatory treatment received in a school for the elite is worth exploring, understanding and dissecting. It is important to share the observation that, while reading through the chapter, one can clearly see that in everything the author did, God was always part of his situational analysis. God's teachings took over whatever negative actions he did that ultimately led him to the path of repentance and subsequent spiritual love.

Part II guides the reader to a higher level of the author's maturity as he continued to explore the mysteries of life relative to his acceptance of Satan's invitations. The citations of the scriptures perfectly timed with the occurrence of certain events, makes one realize the need to study more the Holy Bible.

It takes someone like the author to be able to cite at the right time the teachings from the life of Jesus Christ. His love for the blessed Virgin was clearly depicted on the time he spent to have her gold crown re-constructed into one worthy of the Queen of heaven and earth. How he shared stories and real-life events to explain the concepts of re-incarnation, ghosts and omens are most interesting and truly worthwhile reading.

This can even lead the reader to contemplate on the extent of his own knowledge and appreciation of the Lord's life and how particularly Confessions can help prepare one for a place in heaven. Reading the book will make one realize how little we know about God and how much more we have to do to prepare ourselves for eternity in Heaven.

Chapter II gives a great challenge to the readers' acceptance of the inadequacy of one's spiritual knowledge, exposure and level of understanding. After reading the book, the message is clear … it is high time to go back and understand what God wants you to do for Him, enough to prepare for an eternity of happiness in God's kingdom … simply by reading the Holy Bible and living its teachings.

Jose C. Gatchalian, PhD and
Miflora M. Gatchalian, PhD
May 2019

ACKNOWLEDGMENTS

I extend my *SPECIAL THANKS* to Hon. Gerald Smith, May Ann Kuick, Joe Alvar, and Drs. Pete & Miflora Gatchalian.

&

Thanks to Tony Abear, my SOE (son on earth) for being in charge of the production of this book and Grace Abear, my grandniece for compiling and editing the manuscript.

From Left: Grace, Elmer, and Tony
(July 2018, Niagara Falls, NY, USA)

Thank you to the book illustrators, Joel Gatchalian for the drawings and Alton & Alette Abear for the book cover design and design interpretation (see ILLUSTRATORS).

TABLE OF CONTENTS

PART I: CHILDHOOD FOIBLES & MISCHIEFS
           GROWING UP IN A LARGE FAMILY............................. 1

How My Life Began at Conception 2

Our Father 8

The Story of My Slit Eye 11

A Black Girl from Africa.. 14

The Different Skin Colors Created by God........................ 19

My Childhood Foibles and Mischiefs 22

One Memorable Christmas Day (of Crime & Punishment) 37

My Second Spring's Life 42

PART II: MY OLD AGE IS A GIFT FROM GOD FOR ME 43

The Green Meadow 44

My Old Age Is a Gift from God 45

A Song for My Dad 53

Dad, My Natural Guide 54

Who Was Dad's Natural Guide? 57

The Up Bringing of Papa Anoy 60

Our Lady of Lourdes 61

St. Michael's Monastery 64

The Omens 65

The "Road Less Taken" 67

My Journey to Priesthood 69

My Path to Study Medicine 71

Life at South Western University 74

What Happened at Cebu Institute of Medicine? 76

Predestination 78

God's Providence 80

A Lingering Light of Hope 81

Then, Lucifer Came 83

Reflection of My Padre Pio's Visit 91

The Benefit of Confession 93

The Story of Our Lady's Golden Crown of Fatima 96

A State of Limbo 104

Perhaps the Reason I Live Longer 109

Of Dogs and Ground Hog 110

On Ground Hog 116

I am a Ground Hog 117

My Angel in Human Form 118

WHAT READERS SAY 119

ILLUSTRATORS 123

ABOUT THE AUTHOR 124

THE FAMILY PORTRAIT

The Abear Family

(Front row from left: Elmer, Johnny, Emilio, Maria, Juan, Querubin, Jesus;
Back row from left: Mithras, Uriel, Cesar, Carmencita, Alfredo, Loreto, Ernesto, Romeo)

PART I:

CHILDHOOD FOIBLES & MISCHIEFS
GROWING UP IN A LARGE FAMILY

How My Life Began at Conception

I confess to you, my brothers and sisters: 1st, the fun, the laughter and issues of life, growing up in a large family. 2nd, my childhood mischiefs which by its very nature are sinful and some foible's incidents which, I believe, are harmless act of childhood foolishness.

Anyway, let me introduce to you in satire my knowledge as a Doctor of GP, Ob-Gyn as to how scientifically our life started on earth: As an act of my Dad's love with Mom we found ourselves in her womb, about 6 million of us, Sperms. Have you heard about Monty's song *(1983, video), "Every Sperm is Sacred."* So, don't waste it into the ground, not blessed by God.

Just as ½ + ½ makes only 1 and so were we, 6 million Sperms, each had only ½ life, searching for one Egg's ½ life to form 1 life.

Due to Mom's increasing luteinizing hormone brought about by her ovulation, about the 14th day of her menstrual cycle, her Egg from the follicle of her ovary found its way down into her Fallopian tube and settled on its mid, waiting for Mr. Sperm.

At the upper part of her womb there were two left and right tubes, called the Fallopian tubes. (Our map was accurate). I chose the right tube while others had helped themselves at the left side.

We immediately saw her Egg, not far from us. *"Oh boy,"* I gasped: she was very beautiful, radiant and sparkling like the sun setting against the monstrance of the West. Excited we moved in, tiptoeing like Arthropod.

Though she was so near yet she seemed far away from my heart, among 6 million aspirants, petrified with filial fear and yet delighted at this amazing sight of the Egg. In fairness to Monty's song should I sing, *"Every Egg is Sacred?"* It was not easy competing generally for one Egg. To win her, it was like winning a 649 Jackpot.

After heavy competition of skill and power for us to lay bare for her choice, I won her admiration. She opened her gate and cellular membrane at the border to prevent others from breaking in.

Can you imagine that among the 6 million Sperms she chose and accepted me? Where did the other Sperms go? I heard Dad's song: *"Sacrificial as they were, they just lie, and they die there like heroes do."*

I continued a dreamy symphony, *"Are you warm, are you real, my Mona Lisa. Art thou not the ivory stone painted by Michelangelo that has come to life just for me?"*

We loved and embraced each other, two halves in the process of fertilization along with our DNAs, a kind of sacrificial love to give up ourselves to form one complete human being: this is where my life began, the very moment of my conception.

Save for my nourishment, I was independent from Dad and Mom. For my identity in the world outside, I was provided by Mom and Dad my own DNA. I rolled in, similarly like a chicken egg from the mid Fallopian tube down into Mom's womb. Just as the soil made a mustard seed grow, so was I, growing in Mom's womb.

I had my own heart that swung like a pendulum, mind that could imagine the impossible dream, one body and soul to be happy and to wonder about the mystery of my own existence.

For my own nourishment, I had a cord on my belly bottom. I connected my placenta on the upper part of Mom's womb so it would not stray on my way out, besides giving me a wider room to move and baby fashion, kicking around.

My placenta was like a machine which tried to purify what was good or what was bad into my body and soul. In 5-8 days, I became a Morula, then later an embryo and finally a fetus.

For my sex preference (I did not choose) a click in my Mom's brain (without her awareness) like an Ipad around 5-6 months in the womb someone decided whether I would be heterosexual or homosexual. I was heterosexual. I did not know how I would behave later among my peers. You will find that out as you read further.

Inside this womb, barring complications, from inside or outside, I stayed for 9 months, swimming with great delight in Mom's sea of fluid until I would be ready to take my first breath of air, to expand my 6 lobes of lungs into action, getting ready to be delivered into the world of make-believe.

Anytime when I was within the womb especially on the 6th month, a measles virus could cause allegedly a harelip as it was in the case of Brod Ondo's son named, Dennis. To prevent this, it appears a measles vaccine could have stopped this kind of complication.

It was said that Brod Ondo believed that a clean-cut mid-way at his wife's private part was not made while giving birth, especially since it was her firstborn child. By simply pulling Dennis' big head, it turned both sides of his Mom's private part. Since this was a home delivery, a scoop could not be applied. The latter could have prevented the laceration of both sides of Ondo's wife's private part.

Besides measles, abortion within my 9 months could be another possibility as one of the 'man made complications' during pregnancy. In England they even named it "artificial" abortion. If my Mom wanted me aborted, a doctor could have just as easily inserted some instrument (as it had been done to some women who wanted an abortion) and I would have been a dead Duck even before my time of arrival.

I cannot imagine how painful it would have been for me to know later, perhaps in another life that I had been aborted by my Mom all because she wanted either to save her own life or to stop having more children. Some Lawyers say that Moms have more right to live a more comfortable life with less children than a child that is yet to be born. And pregnancy due to rape or incest that God allowed is no exception.

Anyway, Thank God, my Mom did not abort me. Dad and Mom, in spite of great financial difficulties taking care of 10 children ahead of me, decided that I had the right to live even if it meant a more difficult life for them. I was spared from being aborted, which could have been an act of "murder" according to the belief of "Pro Life" people.

*

Abortion

It was legalized in the United States after the Supreme Court decided on Roe Vs. Wade in 1973. One of the major arguments for legalization was the prevention of back door abortions which they claimed could cause a high incidence of mortality for either baby or mother.

At this point, it may be argued that there were not enough study or research done regarding abortion legalization, since statistics show that legalized abortion had, in fact, resulted to higher mortalities than before legalization.

The fight over this issue between "Pro Life" and "Pro Choice" is still on-going. For instance, every January of the year, about a million people participating in the "March for Life" would walk to the White House, pleading for the life of the unborn.

The "March for Life" was viewed favorably by President Bush such that from his window he delivered an inspirational talk in response to the marchers. Later, he even ordered withdrawal of funds for the "Planned Parenthood" program that supported abortion.

However, during the term of President Obama, an apparent supporter for abortion was shown such that during the "March for Life", President Obama did not even look out perhaps from his window to witness the March for life.

Furthermore, he restored the funding for the "Planned Parenthood" program. It seems, he favored more the death of a child in the mother's womb over the right of a mother to keep her baby.

Despite all these, I have a strong feeling that Roe's appeal made last July 20, 2003 to reverse the decision to legalize abortion, might eventually prevail. Or the metaphorical statement of Wage before he died, *"I am Roe"* might be construed as a plea for reversal (Internet).

Probably, the reason why Dad and Mom did not have me aborted was that, based on the way they lived, they had placed their trust fully in God's hands. Because of this complete trust, they were able to withstand the many trials and difficulties of raising a large family and they continued to survive with God's grace and love.

*

Our Father

To give credence to my good father I recited this verse before him. I wanted him to hear it before he would pass away into the other world. This verse entitled *"Our Father"* was also recited by my late brother Jess during our Father's interment on April 17, 1975:

Our Father

We have realized from the years that passed
*   about the care and love you have given us.*
Once we were children and did wrong
*   you never spared the rod.*
It maybe, that like me
*   not all branches were growing straight.*

But surely, nobody could do better
*   than what you did.*
Once we were sick and weak
*   you stayed beside our bed*
To give us the comfort of an Angel.

Then, when world war II broke-out,
*   like a hen with her chicks under her wings*
You brought us to Kansuhi,
*   beyond the reach of butchers*
Who cut people themselves in the cover of darkness

The war had taken away the best from us,
*   we had to go somewhere else*
Where the pasture was greener as in Davao
*   and there was hope for a brighter tomorrow.*
Yet amidst the brightness and gaiety
*   Binugao could give,*

There were times when we got lost
*   in our purple forebodings.*
You did not only show us the light
*   but showed us through the narrow road as well.*

There were times too that our family's peace
*   was shaken by madness to its root:*
We acted like rebels, we lost respect for one another.

In all those stormy nights, you stood like an Oak tree
*   with understanding that was almost divine*
With compassion, that was almost Christ like
And so, we endured the agony and as we did
*   we saw your 'wisdom'*
Saw our false obsessions which appeared like
*   a picture of our sheer ingratitude.*

You will never know the days and nights
    we spent in silence,
Suturing gaping wounds of broken selves
    that in due time made us less judgmental,
    less ruthless.

Indeed, forgive us, for our self-righteousness
    we fell short of what was hidden beyond
    the horizon of your foresight.

Now, we are old and gray, but you stand before us,
    not a symbol of weakness
But of strength and vigor that had silenced
    so many gales in the sea of life
And came out victorious.

Sponsored by the KofC
    Pope Paul VI rewarded you in 1969
as one of the ten most outstanding
    families throughout the Philippines.

Indeed, your image shall in no time
    be swallowed into the mouth of forgetfulness
but will remain, beyond the limit of time
    an enduring ideal
That we are proud to pass on to our next generation,
    So, help us God!

*

The Story of My Slit Eye

This was worse than the harelip of Dennis, but I was not cantankerous Unfortunately, I was born into this world, with a slit eye on my left. This made me look ugly. But, in spite of my defect Mom and Dad lavished me with their love and care.

My Mom said I was the most fair-looking baby instead of being the most fair-looking "ugly" (in my own mind). I even got the modest word to describe myself as "ugly." May be because of my "slit eye" I was born not likely to be an honest person and not for what I should be.

Growing up with a "slit eye" among my peers, life was not easy. I was proud that all my brothers were good looking. I wished in my little heart I would have been like them. But their fortune was my misfortune for it had made me feel "ugly" and different from the normal people around me including my so-called friends.

While my brothers could easily choose a beautiful girl for their date, especially on weekends, I had to stay home moping and almost cursing over my fate, the ugliness of my own physical defect. There were times when I got naughty that affected others.

For instance, instead of keeping my defect a secret, they glared at me by shouting "pikot" (half-opened eye in Cebuano) … "pikot" …. loud and repeatedly. It hurt me so much, I felt like cursing them to high Heavens wishing them to go to hell! At these times, pride in myself would go almost to nothingness! How I hated the word "pikot" such that if it was a smaller kid jeering me…

I would have blackened his eye to stop him from calling me "pikot" ever again. With the big kids, although I was not afraid of them, still I avoided fighting them lest instead of one pickot I might have two.

Besides, why should I allow myself to lose? I have already lost the beauty of my left eye, why get some more black eye? I was terribly defensive of my perceived ugliness. But what can I do … this is the only face and eye that I possess?

If you were like me what would you have done? *"Thank God?"* and I self-responded with a whispered, *"Yes, I will"* since God is very generous! In His kindness, He did not create me to be a wolf, bellowing as if cursing the moonlight or a giant bat that scares children during Halloween's night.

Yes, I will thank God despite my "slit eye" for He must have given this to me for a purpose which only He knows at this time. Perhaps at the right time in the future, if I am good, He might make me understand.

I asked my Dr. Brod Johnnie why I looked like this? He said that perhaps it happened because of our Mom's expressed unusual desires during her pregnancy… we call *Pangala* in Visayan or *"Paglili"* in Pilipino.

During those times in her early pregnancy, our Mom would not let a day pass without looking at our neighbor, Eldy Puerto who was then called "Eldy *nga Pikot*." (Eldy with left-eye half-closed).

In many instances, to entice him to come near her, she would bribe him with candies and at times offer him money. She felt most comfortable with "Eldy *nga Pikot*" around her.

Boy, how unlucky I was being in Mom's womb and could not do anything about her urgent desires, that translated itself into her own baby's being *"pikot."* Could you believe that? I could not and will not. But still it happened, and unfortunately it happened, to me!

So, whenever I saw Eldy Puerto, oh, how I hated him and even wished he would slip on a banana pill and would end two Pickots instead of one. Or if he were not around, I would have been a very handsome guy with my fair skin, handsome face with my right eye tainted brown and bluish, an inheritance from my generous Spanish grandparent, Fr. Molina, a Missionary from Spain.

*

A Black Girl from Africa

By the way, do you know the story about a black girl, being born in the midst of 14 boys with Spanish temperament? The old traditional wisdom was to let my 3 older brothers, Emelio, Alfredo and Johnnie to work under the heat of the Summer sun for 7 days without salary and what's more they had also too fast.

Well, when Mom got pregnant everybody expected that after 8 boys in a row, this time it would be a girl. They were right… it was a girl! What was so interesting was that while all my brothers looked Caucasian of Spanish descent, she appeared like a *Molato*, a mixture of black and white. I considered her a black girl because I thought this would make her more dignified than being labeled as *Molato*.

Dad who believed in re-incarnation thought that she came from Africa and was re-incarnated in the Philippines so that she could get a brown skin. Unfortunately, she got a *Molato*, heh, heh. Not so funny for her but very funny to us brothers.

Imagine, a *"black girl"* among the midst of Caucasians, heh, heh. This has nothing to do with racism. In fact, at that time, we never heard of "racism" in the Philippines. She looked unique, beautiful and nothing more like her around. No sarcasm intended.

I called her *"Chita"* named after Chita, the monkey who adopted a baby that survived a plane crash. *Chita* took good care of him and treated him like her own baby by nourishing him from her breast milk. He was called *Tarzan*.

We, kids, wondered why *Tarzan* did not get black having been nourished from the breast milk of a black hairy monkey. We thought all along that the skin color "white" meant stronger, but not necessarily more superior than "black."

Also, "Chita" was taken from the root word for Carmencita worthy to be called, *"the black monkey"* from a movie I saw in Argao's (town of Cebu, Philippines) municipal park in 1946, entitled *"Tarzan's Secret Treasure."* People born in the 1930's and 40's will remember this movie.

Carmencita reminded me of the monkey-mother of Tarzan called Chita. I thought it was pure coincidence that the end part of her name rhymed like Chita. No malice intended, it is *Pag bo-ot sa Dios* or God's will.

Thus, whenever Carmencita bullied me because she was big with black hairy arms, behaved like a husky big boy, I called her *"Chita, the monkey eating eagle."* Oh, how she would get so upset. I had to run and hide behind Mom's skirt for protection. And she would say, *"Wait, Pikot, until Mom is out of town and you will see."*

And I would answer back: *"Of course, you can see me in the dark because I am white, and you are black."* And she would get furious showing her monkey's canine teeth. Grrr!

I told Dad that I did not believe in re- incarnation as taught to me by the Jesuit fathers at the Ateneo de Davao. He said, whether I believe it or not I was a product of a re-incarnation from Spain. So, he said, *"Be thankful to Fr. Molina for his generosity."* It was rumored that he fathered 24 all male-kids in Iloilo, Philippines. Indeed, Fr. Molina's progeny started a village, then a town. So, if one aborts a child you wipe out a village. Do you understand that, *"Pro-choice which is no choice for a baby in the womb"*?

I told my Dad, that Christ said that a *"Man is born once and is judged"* (John 16.8-11). He argued that Christ also said, *"Unless you become a little child you cannot enter the Kingdom of Heaven" (Mathew 18:3) "How is that?"* I replied.

"Have you not met a person who is born honest? It was because in his previous life he was a thief." (That hit me because I was a thief in the house). Would he also think, I said to myself, that since I had the passion to eat bones that I reincarnated from the dog? Oh, boy! To me, re-incarnation was not getting any better.

At that stage of my brain's intellectual capacity I could not argue against him. But it did not mean I accepted it. I hated the idea of being born again with my "slit eye". It could even get worse if I were reincarnated in Japan where some have eyes which are both slit eyes. Excuse me my Japanese friends, no malice intended.

Although Dad believed in re-incarnation, he remained a good Catholic. He would attend Mass, received Holy Communion and regularly went to confession. *"Dad,"* I told him, *"You are a perfect man. I never heard you tell a lie, never saw you angry, in spite of our being unruly, you remained unruffled, slept well while we were out at night, returned home, drunk and sometimes bloody from a fight. You must be on the 7th year of your re-incarnation so that when you die you go straight to Heaven."* He laughed.

He said that Christ did not come to save good people because they were already saved (Luke 5. 27-31) to mention a few out of so many like Padre Pio, Pope John Paul VI, Mo. Theresa of Calcutta. Christ said he came only for sinners so that he can forgive their sins and get their souls redeemed. This way, they could reign with him in Heaven forever and ever.

Whenever people did not understand what He was saying he said it in parables. In this case He, as a good Shepherd, left 99 of his white sheep and went out to look for his lost black sheep in the forest. He found and brought him back to join his 99-white sheep.

What lesson do we learn here? Those who have not heard this parable obviously have not learned anything. Those who have heard but do not believe, it's probably because they do not need salvation since they are the good chosen people whom Jesus mentioned in some of His talks. All they can do, as I mentioned earlier, is to give something more so that they may gain a higher place in Heaven.

By the way, I don't know if my mother believed in re-incarnation, but she was a witness of my Father's incredible power. Mom told me that in 1939 when there was a big carnival in Cebu City Dad told her to select a number from a big rolling wheel with numbers. People turned the wheel and if it stopped at say 100, they get the price. Remember this show on TV?

So, every time Mom told Dad to say a new number the wheel pointer would stop at Dad's chosen number. Mom said, *"Since you have the gift to predict the winning number, why don't we gamble for that number and win the price?"* Dad answered, *"If I will do that, I will lose my gift."*

I wondered where did Dad learn about re-incarnation? I noticed that in his library he had all kinds of books, like for instance… the "Holy Bible," where all our names were written, date of birth and place. He also had "The Imitation of Christ," by Thomas E Kempis, and many others. He also must have been reading the 6 volumes of Madame Blavatsky's *"The Secret Doctrine."*

Although I tried to read some of Dad's books, I merely learned that on the middle but deep into the Nile River was the "Mother of all flowers", the source of many blessings for all people living along the Jordan River (one of the tributaries of the Nile river I think).

It is known that Christ was baptized in this river which later became the source of abundant blessings for sinners during His time and even to date. Moses floated over this lengthy Nile River too. What design in Heaven linked these incidents?

*

The Different Skin Colors Created by God

In the Philippines, it is a nationally known and or accepted folklore, a fictional story that at the time God created the first man. He took him out of the oven too early and the man was under-baked, very pale and almost *white*.

Then He tried to produce another man and some people said that God must have gone outside his house to call his dog. It took some time before he found the dog. When he returned to the house to check on his oven, he saw that the man had been overbaked and appeared so dark, almost black.

God also noted, that his hair had curled and looked kinky, but his teeth and sclera remained white. The latter will enable anyone meeting the black man in the dark to see his white teeth and sclera. Thus, if we happened to walk in the dark and meet this man, at least we will know that there is a human being ahead worthy to be loved and respected.

Finally, for the last time God became more careful in watching the baking time to ensure that the finished product will neither be pale nor dark. Thus, at the end of the set baking time, God finally knew he had made the best color of a properly baked man. He opened the oven and lo and behold, He saw a man with the perfect color.

Meeting His expectations was a man who had a very well-controlled skin… *"brown"* neither *"white"* nor *"black"* but a perfect color! This marked the creation of the *"brown"* people and in the Philippines, they are known as Filipinos.

Although Filipinos are generally good looking with such nice brown skin, yet most of them, unlike the Americans and other Caucasians, had flat noses. But, is flat nose worse than the extra huge nose of Cyrano de Vergerac? I wonder.

When some Caucasians grow old, their noses become so prominently big and crooked that it would appear they look like witches!!! Ha, ha ha. No ridicule intended, just trying to reason why many Filipinos have flat noses!

Every morning when no one was around in the house, I would pull-up my nose in front of the mirror hoping it could lengthen and reduce its flatness. Unfortunately, it did not work, today I am still sporting my flat nose with its big wheels on each side… so big that if you look thru my nostrils you might even see my brain, oh, ya ya yay!

As a consequence of my efforts to lengthen my nose, my turbinate got displaced, which no EENT (Eye, Ear Nose Throat) doctor could fix. To date, I am suffering from rhinitis…giving good business to decongestant manufacturers. Don't you think I should be compensated?

When sometime decongestant did not work on my nose my exhale smelled bad, not to mention my bad breath enough that my good wife would graciously stay away from me especially at night when we are in bed! Oh boy, she missed my nightingale, heh, heh.

Talking of skin color…what about the *yellow skin* man associated with the Chinese? Would any Chinese have a good answer regarding their skin color? Could it be that God could not put him in the oven because they were *yellow* when He called them!

In this regard, some Chinese thought God was unfair, because walking with a yellow skin is not a joke …imagine it! They could be mistaken as somebody who has a problem with their "bag of insulin." How some yellow-skinned ones wished God would put them in the oven and then open it early so their skin would be *white.*

Anyway, maybe God made the different colors of people's skin to make people differentiate from each other, perhaps out of the vanity. Some people criticize other people's skin, oftentimes degrading them, up to a point when they appear "racists" and may be missed the color of their souls…white for grace or black for sin. But this has nothing to do with one's physical skin.

*

My Childhood Foibles and Mischiefs

Now, get ready! I confess to you my childhood foibles and mischiefs which might be disturbing and not acceptable to your personal sensitivity since they are, in fact, salacious or too much for your holy soul to handle, please proceed to item No. 2 instead.

If, however, you have the courage, perhaps with a mortified spirit then I encourage you to read on and I beg your forgiveness so that, may be, you can still pray for me? An 8-year-old child who is expected to be innocent.

Excuse me, but at that age, I was no longer an innocent one…so very unlike Padre Pio who, as a child was playing with Angels. In fact, even before age 8 I was already played with the devils… some, I felt were actually inside me while others were right outside my closest environment. For example, instead of using my conscience to choose what was right, I would prefer to create my own conscience and purposely did the wrong thing, largely for the satisfaction of ego's carnality.

Although I knew I was the captain of my body and the master of my soul, yet I felt I was not pre-determined, like Padre Pio and all the other good people, to go Heaven. I believed I was born a sinner who needed a Savior, otherwise I would go directly to Hell.

If only I won't die, I won't believe in Hell but would be thankful to God instead. The same thing with what Brod Lading told me when we were growing up, he said, *"Brod, if I don't believe in God, I would have committed suicide long ago."* It seemed God gave him Lymphoma and died of such cancer of the RBC at age 77. Lucky 7 for Heaven is not it?

Do you believe in Hell? Padre Pio said, *"You will believe in Hell when you will be there!"* If I would be in Hell that would be too late for me to return to earth to undo the wrong things I had done. All I could do is wait, for God's mercy not for his justice as we daily pray, *"I believe in God...the resurrection of the body and life everlasting. Amen"* *(Nicean Creed).*

(A). *"Thou shall not commit adulterous act."*

I confess to you, my sinful experience. I played with girls in Grade II class, yanking their skirts during recess time to try to see our differences. They shouted with anger while I felt excited especially to see and discover our great difference.

This behavior could surely explain why I was born a heterosexual, attracted to the opposite sex and wanted to make love with them even as a child. But, come to think of it, weren't my actions very 'natural' for children of my age? Look who is talking?

Another cute incident should be recounted about my childhood foibles. During World War II little girls in our town did not wear panties (for lack of available materials to use) except on Sundays or Holidays of obligation.

And that was the same with us boys who saved our few briefs to wear in church, because according to my older brother, we must respect Jesus in the Blessed Sacrament. Also, for lack of alternatives. Most of us wore the same clothes every day going to school from Monday to Friday. Thus, by Friday we all looked dirty and smelly especially in our armpits.

Until now I don't know the explanation why my armpits left several days unwashed it smells good, so that in the privacy of my room I keep smelling it, oh, how sweat, not to mention my wen. Yet, when it comes from other armpits or wen it is so repugnant.

This sounds to me that my nose by nature is practicing discrimination without my consent. For the love and benefit of others we buy deodorant to keep it under control. Do you have any scientific explanation, the vanity of my armpits and my butt?

Talking again about conscience. Although I believe I do not own my conscience, yet my free will tells me I have the right to use it according to my own appreciation of the situation. Hence, whenever I chose to do the wrong thing, even when I knew what was right, I would convince myself that doing wrong was still alright! Perhaps during our time or even today, there are children who still think and behave the same way as I did then.

I remember, when I was just a little child, it was quite vague to me what virtues could come out by doing good to others. It seemed doing good was a very hard thing to follow because it meant I will have to think of other's feelings. As a child I believed that thinking of others was not only time-consuming, it was also very boring.

It was always clear to me then what kind of "vices" could result from doing bad things, but these "vices" gave me much "pleasure" and complete enjoyment. Doing bad is so easy to accomplish, with so much thrill in the process of performance, although at times, accompanied with much risk. My experiences in the next section are actual examples of the things I knew were bad, yet I continued doing them despite the risks I had to take.

Old woman asking people to help find her lost 5 peso bill

(B). *"Thou shall not steal."*

At the risk of getting spanked by my Dad, if I was caught stealing my Mom's coins, I deliberately and frequently stole her coins. On many instances, I got caught stealing Mom's coins and I suffered the consequences…Dad's strong lashes on my buttocks! Boy, how painful it was but my style was to shout, *"Dad, enough, I am already dead."* It worked! Most of the time, I usually escaped with less than ten lashes heh, heh, heh.

The pleasure of stealing was far above and beyond the risk of getting caught. Any known corporal punishment was no deterrent because I knew I could handle anything inflicted on me. I loved and enjoyed doing what I knew was bad especially when I gained something for myself like having stolen money.

I stole because I could never ask money from either Dad or Mom since they have nothing to spare from all the money needed to take care of 13 living children! So, the easiest and only way I could get money was to steal from them.

Knowing that I had been stealing, my older brother, would jokingly tell me that when I grow older I could easily qualify as a member of *"Alibaba and the 40 thieves."* At that time, I already knew that the Alibaba Gang stole money from the rich to be used for the good of the poor.

Thus, being their member, is a great honor and privilege and I felt so good to see this as my future! Meanwhile, I needed to continue doing my petty thievery (*"kupit"* in Pilipino) to improve my capabilities! Like Alibaba I should share to others what I had stolen.

For example, my older brother Cesar would ask me to steal from my Dad's cabinet. I must obey him, otherwise he would cross his fingers and that meant the end of our friendship. You see, because my hand was small, I could easily slip my fingers into my Dad's cabinet and then reach out for the money kept there.

Money always made my Brod Cesar happy and I felt so good of my generosity, pleasing him. Later, I found out that he gambled at the town plaza betting on a "jumping ball between red and blue."

Soon, I followed his good example. I took over the gambling business. But unluckily, most of the time, I lost more than win, and this prompted me to steal even more to overcome my losses. It was really bad for the business but good for stealing more and more. Then, I also decided to steal not only from my parents but also from others for bigger amounts. Thus, I began to plan on how to steal from other people.

The occasion for more stealing opportunities came, when in 1945 the G.I. U.S. Armed forces brought into our basement rations as aid from the generous people from America for the poor people. During liberation people would gather in front of our house in Media, Argao (Cebu-Philippines) and wait for their share of the U.S. rations.

As I watched these poor people who were gathered at the door of our home waiting for it to open, I thought that stealing from their pockets would be a good idea. When the door was opened, people rushed (lining up did not work here) pushing each other going down to the basement. I also went down with them and soon I got mixed into the crowd.

The back pockets of men appeared tight and I could not risk inserting my hand into them. Then, I saw an old woman with her bag wide open. I looked at her face while I dug into her open bag and got hold of a paper money. I quickly ran upstairs with the money and waited behind the window to see what the old woman would do after she would discover her money was gone.

Ahhh, there she was, the old white haired woman was crying and begging others for help in the search for her lost money. She said, that she lost her 5-peso bill, her only treasure which she saved throughout the war years.

As she continued the search with tears in her eyes she explained that she promised her grand-daughter she would take care of buying the white cloth to be made into her wedding gown. She said they have no other source of funds to cover this need.

She went outside away from the crowd and sat on a big stone in the corner asking people passing by if they could help her recover her 5 peso bill which might have fallen from her bag. She took my heart out. I regretted what I had done, but I did not have the nerve to lie to her that I found it on the floor at the basement.

I was afraid she might accuse me of stealing the money and report me to the Police. Imagine me, the son of the Town Mayor (well-known for his honesty), being accused as a thief? I could not handle that.
X
I went out when there were no more people around and proceeded to the stone where she sat in the corner, then placed the money under the stone. I had hoped that tomorrow she would return to that corner, look around the stone where she sat and then find the money. But days and days passed and she never showed up. I decided to take the money, placed it behind the glass door of our cabinet and hoped that someone would soon find and claim it.

The next day the glass was broken and the money was gone. For a while I thought that one of the members of the Alibaba and the 40 thieves had stolen it. But later, I learned who it was that took the money… it was Boy Ernesto., another older brother.

When my younger brother Loreto came, he felt sad for me when I told him that I lost my money. I pretended to be so upset but in my heart I was thankful, that Boy Ernesto had kept the money which helped me put my mind at peace, heh, heh. heh *I resolved then and there never again to steal.*

My resolve not to steal anymore was not mainly to help purify my mind or to put it at peace but more so because of the realization followed by acceptance that my *childhood misdemeanor* is actually just a part of growing-up and should now be forgiven and forgotten.

Red luscious "tambis" fruit that attracted Elmer

(C). *"Thou shall not commit covetousness."*

I confess to you that in Argao, in front of our convenience store was a huge market building. It was usually empty after five in the evening when all the vendors packed up their things and went home.

After five o'clock we kids would gather to play "hide and seek", one of our childhood games. I saw one pretty girl among our group, named Rosita. To play this game, each person pairs with another, shake hands with the partner, then after saying *"papel, grunting, bato"* release the shake, the quickly, using hand gesture mimic either a paper *(papel)* which can cover a stone, scissor *(gunting)* which can cut a paper or stone *(bato)* which can destroy a scissor.

The remaining loser, after hand-shaking with all possible pairs, would become the "IT" and would have to cover his/her eyes leaning against a post or tree and count 1 to 10. Meanwhile, all the others would run to find a place to hide. After the count of 10, the IT should search for all the others. Everyone must be able to touch the post or tree, where the IT stood counting, to be considered SAFE before being found by the IT.

This time I intentionally wanted to lose because I had in mind to find Rosita and kiss her rosy cheeks. I successfully lost, so I leaned on the post pretending to have closed my eyes although I could still see between my fingers where Rosita went to hide.

At the count of 10, I saw her still looking for a place to hide. I ran very fast to catch her but when I was about to hold her, I hit a box of sand (used by people when spitting). I stumbled twice and injured my shin bone on my left leg. I was bleeding from a slash on my shin bone about 4 inches in length. I could actually see my bone.

Until now at my age (82 years) the scar on my left leg is still visible, perhaps a symbol of God's wrath for my wrong intentions. In case, you are interested to see my big scar I can show you. Such intended act (my desire to kiss) which was not completed can be considered a venial sin. My scar is, thus, a picture of Hell on earth which would remain with me forever unto my grave.

Elmer falling on his back from the "tambis" tree as his eyes got diverted to the provocative pose of Nena on the stairs.

(D). *"Thou shalt not commit adultery."*

Whenever I felt bored in my Grade III class, under Mrs. Amparo, I would volunteer to clean her house instead of our classroom. I loved to clean her house because in her front yard, she had a big *Tambis* tree (like an Apple tree in the Philippines). It bore fruits which, when ripe are almost heart-shaped red in color, very sweet and juicy to eat.

When I and Rogelio, Mrs. Amparo's son, arrived in their house, our playmate Nena was already there, waiting for us. This time after we finished cleaning the house, I decided to climb the *Tambis* tree and feast on all the ripe red fruits I could find there, rather than play with Nena.

But then, right across the tree, I saw Nena sitting upstairs with her knees wide open, as if inviting me to watch her "open sesame." When I was about to grasp the sweetest *Tambis,* I could not help but get distracted over the view freely open to me…Nena!

Curiosity got the better of me and I tried to bend my head very low so I could see what was between her thighs. As my eyes journeyed between her legs, into a no man's land, my heart began beating wildly and my ears were getting hot.

Then, just as I was about to pull the 'red *Tambis*,' I did not realize that I had bent so low causing me to lose my balance. I fell like Icarus on a grassy knoll, back first…big thud on the ground.

Although I could hardly breathe because of the impact, I tried to stand up macho-like. I saw Nena running down the stairs and she said, *"Are you alright?"* I answered, *"Not so, I just missed the red Tambis."* And she laughed.

For sure, she did not know the adulterous mind I had on her red Tambis that I missed, heh, heh! NOTE: Jesus said *if you look at a woman with adultery on your mind you have already committed. So*, how could I be saved?

(E). ***"Thou shall love your neighbor as you love yourself."***

In our convenience store, named: "Jacinta Enterprises" we also had a corn and rice mill where I worked. Usually, after working in the rice mill I would feel so tired that I would sleep behind a pile of boxes and sacks of rice.

But this time I overslept. Every day before going home, Dad and Mom would lock the door of the store. Thus, I found myself all alone inside the locked store and had no other recourse but to pass the night there.

It must have been 8 o'clock in the evening because I could hear from our neighbor's store radio, my favorite Filipino-Cebuano show, "Ang Batang Kahibulongan" (The Wonder Boy). Outside, it already started to rain. At home, Mom and Dad did not notice my absence, which was not surprising because all my eight brothers and a sister were at home, so I was not missed..

The following morning when I woke up. I did not want to wait for the store to open at 9 o'clock because I was already very hungry and wanted to go home. I looked up to the store chimney and observed that it would be possible for me to slip underneath and out onto the roof.

I was right and I was out on the roof. Across our store I saw *Amang* (A Cebuano word describing a person with verbal disability), whose real name I never know. In Argao (town of Cebu), during those times, if one had a defect, that person gets named by that defect, like me being called "*Pikot*" because of my half-closed left eye.

They were not cruel, they simply enjoyed coining words to label a person based on their obvious physical defect. So, this man was named *Amang*. He was dumb but not deaf. He was eating a sandwich at the time I saw him.

From atop the roof, I made my water. *Amang* looked-up and smiled at me, his face seemed right on target. So, I directed my "fireman's hose" slowly but surely towards him and he got so upset especially when his sandwich got wet. I did not mind his being mad, I knew he was afraid of me. In fact, I bullied him many times before.

I continued to enjoy directing my "hose" towards him and he got more wet from the breeze even though I was already running out of water from my human "hose". He got "baptized" by the breeze and he was really fuming mad. This made me laugh at him all the more. If this is an example of my love for neighbor, it might be considered just part of my *childhood foibles* while growing-up… heh, heh, heh !!!

As I started to walk on the galvanized-iron roof, I noticed it was slippery and though I tried to balance myself, there was nothing I could hold on to, so I fell from the roof, back first on the table directly below.

The impact was so strong that I could hardly breath. But I managed to go down from the table and while doing so, I heard *Amang* laughing. He had the last laugh. I angrily looked at him with my clinched fist and he vanished out of my sight. I laughed, heh, heh, heh,,.actually I had the last laugh but with much pain.

(F). *"Thou shall not smoke."*

I saw my brothers smoking. I did not know how good it must be for them to see their money go in smoke. I said to myself I would rather buy a Hersey chocolate than smoke.

Anyhow, my curiosity about cigarettes was strongly heightened such that one afternoon, I stole one pack of "Piedmont" cigarettes containing 20 sticks from our Convenience Store. I went home and smoked the whole pack under the coconut tree near our house. I enjoyed looking at the smoke going up into the sky.

After I consumed the 20 sticks I stood up to go home. I felt very dizzy and walked like a drunken kid. I started to throw up. I almost did not reach home but I managed to enter into my room and threw up some more. From that day on, I resolved never to smoke again and that resolution had been kept to this day even now at my age of 82 year

*

Fr. Webster whacking Elmer's exposed butt for the perceived mischief he had done

One Memorable Christmas Day
(of Crime & Punishment)

One of my unforgettable experiences at the Ateneo de Davao, when I was yet in second year high school, was one that happened to me one Christmas day. At that time, Fr. Webster, SJ was our "Father Discipline," known as the tough former U.S. Marine who fought in World War II.

It is even possible that he could be one of those G.I.'s in 1946 who slept in our house because there were no more Japanese soldiers to shot since they ran away weeks before their arrival.

Anyway, during Christmas day at the Ateneo, Fr. Webster like a Dictator, circulated a memorandum that no firecrackers are allowed to be exploded in the gym or elsewhere in the area.

Unfortunately, a firecracker exploded and everybody ran away from the scene. Fr. Webster caught me and in spite of my pleading, that *"I did not do it"* he still collared me into a room for the beating punishment.

It was possible that from my pleading he felt I was actually innocent since he found no evidence to prove that I was guilty ... so he reconsidered my plea of not guilty. Then he said, *"Ok, I will spare you."* I said to myself, *"Heh, heh, my truthfulness spared me.*

Fr. Webster brought me outside and made me stand near the flagpole where several cars were parked. Classes resumed. I was alone beside the flagpole. But after about 10 minutes firecrackers started to explode right underneath the cars near the flagpole.

I wanted to run and hide. But my conscience said, *"Why I should I? I did not do it."* Up and down all windows of our school, were smiling faces looking at me. Some must have thought I was such a tough guy to explode firecrackers within the view of everyone!

The attention focused on me was enjoyable. And I felt very proud what I assumed they thought I was a tough guy. From the entrance of the school grounds, came Fr. Webster holding a long wooden ruler, the weapon he use for spanking naughty kids. I was not afraid. I felt calm, after all, I did not do it.

He walked fast, came to me and held my collar. I explained, *"I did not do it. It was a time bomb underneath the car."* He did not even listen to me, he simply sneered at me. Then, I really got nervous. What if my brother Emelio, the school Registrar who paid my tuition fee, would learn about this? The thought was not enjoyable.

He would surely transfer me to a Public School, the school for *"have nots."* Ateneo de Davao was a high school for wealthy people like the family of the Sarena's, the Duterte's, the Oboza's, the Cam's who sent their children to school in private cars.

I was one of the poor who studied at the Ateneo, mainly because I did not want to study in a public school and be among the poor. To have us (I and Brod Lading) enrolled in this school, my Brod Emilio had to pull strings. Unlike the privileged children of wealthy parents who came to school in private cars Brod Lading and I had to take the school bus everyday.

We could not afford the meals sold from the school canteen, so everyday, we had to bring our lunch in a small plastic bag. It contained one boiled egg and rice. During lunch time, Brod Lading and I would eat under the school's bleacher area, a place used for sports activities like the basketball games.

There were times at home, when we made our housemaid, Goring's life miserable by doing mischiefs that bothered her. Later, we discovered in school that our lunch had no boiled egg but rather a smelly dried fish and not rice but just corn grits. We could not complain to Mom because Goring's rank in the house was a lot higher than ours.

One thing funny with Goring I found her making her water every morning facing South. So, politely I asked her why? She said that she was instructed by her father that whenever she passed her water she should face South. This was necessary so that when she would her folks in Bohol (Visayan province near Cebu) her hometown to take her short vacation, she would not lose her way.

And so to continue our life in school like eating our lunch under the bleacher, we noted we had actually two neighbors also eating lunch under the bleacher. These boys were working students. We noted that the only working student, who did not eat under the bleacher, was a Frenchman's son named Armand, who worked in the library.

Armand and I became very close friends and at times, we played basketball together. But I rarely played with him because he was a good shooter and I was not. Losing was not in my vocabulary so to avoid the humiliation of losing I would avoid playing with him. He later became a member of the prestigious basketball team of the Ateneo de Davao.

One thing I did not understand; he called me *Polyphemus*. Working in the library Armand must have learned a lot of good words. As for me, I seldom went to the library. It was a boring place to spend my useful time.

My high school days were only for fun so I managed to fail in two subjects, one was Arithmetic. A Chinaman once told me that 5+5 equals 11 and I believed him and this could be the reason why I failed in our Arithmetic final exam because I answered 5+5 equals 11. I also failed in English, mainly because I did not understand grammar, Visayan (like Cebuano) language does not have grammar, I was later told.

The only excellent grade I had was History. I loved to memorize what happened in the past like the one time great conqueror Napoleon Bonaparte. He was exiled to St. Helena and ultimately killed in Waterloo. Some people say, buried underground, he would be slowly eaten by worms. I did not want to believe that.

Going back to Fr. Webster and the firecracker explosions, I thought he was finally convinced that I was innocent. Yet, he told me to line up with some boys who were punished to walk around the gymnasium. Well, being boys we made foolishness along the line, pushing playfully one another.

Fr. Webster came and pulled 2 boys (one was me). I thought we were the less naughty ones, from the line. But perhaps he was just waiting for the last straw that might break his camel's back and this was it. He brought us inside a class room, locked it.

He then instructed Modesto (the other boy), to bend and hold on the seat of a chair, put his pants down to show the full view of his butts covered with brief and soon the ruler came, whack, whack whack! But before the ruler hit his butt he would shout as if with great pain. He received only 5 lashes.

It was easy viewing my plain uncovered butts, because unlike Modesto, I could not afford a brief. As instructed I bent and held on to a chair seat and soon the ruler came with full strength from the former Marine's force.

Fr. Webster struck with the ruler perhaps with all his might since I could hear the wheezing sound as the ruler struck my naked butt…whack, whack, whack! It was a very painful experience, a punishment for the fire cracker explosion for which I was innocent! He stopped after 9 lashings. I took a punishment for a crime I never committed. *"Do I gain any indulgence for this?"* I thought.

Later, I thought if I had shouted with great pain like Modesto I might have had less lashings. I forgot to do that because I was so preoccupied with the thought that *"I honestly did not do it, why should I be punished"*? Fr. Webster must have greatly enjoyed spanking my butt with his wooden ruler that he eventually got tired and voluntarily gave up after the 9th count.

*

My Second Spring's Life

In part I of my life, I was once a young red Apple hanging in the tree of life at the back of our house in Ogdensburg, New York.

When I was sweet 16 and wild, I was nightly visited by a young Bird of different feathers.

She pinned pecked me the pain and pleasure of her life, not withstanding mine.

Now, a Savior in the order of Melchizedek took a compassionate look at me, a lost teenage, unmasking his covered face with 19 horns saw my soulmate in deep atonement of my misgivings.

Transformed me by His forgiveness into an amazing gorgeous life, like a full-grown Rose among the weeds and Dandelions in the Autumn of my new Second Spring's life.

*

PART II:

MY OLD AGE IS A GIFT
FROM GOD FOR ME

The Green Meadow

In part II of my old age life, I finally fell out of grace from the tree of life into the Green Meadow, the Mediatrix of all graces.

Shall I say, "Too late have I found God thru no merit of my own, but her Motherhood saved me from darkness to light!"

Now, at 83 years old I'm likened into a mere dry old Apple, a cavernous leaf, transformed in the heart of the Green Meadow.

Gracefully, I turn into a full bloom Rose among the weeds and the Dandelions in the Autumn of my anticipated first Spring's life.

Come my first Spring's life, on my knees, I now humbly say, "Thy kingdom come to me thru the Mediatrix of all graces into the open gate of Heaven where my heavenly Father reigns forever." Alleluia!

*

I Confess to You:

My Old Age Is a Gift from God

How can I confess to you the beginning of the end of my 83-year-old life? In simple words, how will I write my past life's true experiences in relationships with you and others and thereby know where I would go next? If this sounds fluffy, don't forget you're dealing with an old man whose long memory might be intact but his short memory, I could hardly remember, "What day is it today?

When I was working as a part time Doctor at the Geriatric Hospital, the first thing I did was to test old folks their orientation. I asked them – what day, time and place is it today? The most common mistake is for them to say, Wednesday when it was Monday. It seems that most old folks (me no exception) tend to look forward like St. Francis Serra rather than backward.

Oftentimes, I would even use this as an excuse for what I should become rather than for what I am. What can I do under this situation? To avoid moving into despair on thinking of the beginning of my end (which I am sure also plagued some seniors), I needed a spiritual model like St. Simon to guide me. For a break, I, in fact, wrote a poem, God's gift of my old age:

My Old Age

My old age
is a gift from God.
believe me, no Seniors like me
deserve it.

Whereas when the chemistry
of my body & mind
was once young,
power & self-interest moved me,
with no regard to right or wrong.

And I asked, at that time,
no Heaven to do it right for me.
Somehow, I survived
into the garbage of old age.

Now when I'm old
my body's chemistry,
not to mention my soul mate
has shrunk further…

Into a dry fetid fettered land
unable to do what salacious
mind I'm still damn drawn into.

One day
thru no merit of my own,
God filtered thru
my unchaste brain
the purity of His heart,

I've become what I owe to be,
A creature of faith, hope & charity,
no more fear of death
neither malice at my old age,
so help me God.

St Simon receiving Baby Jesus from Mother Mary

I then chose St. Simon because he had Prophet Elijah to guide him and who said to him, that at the end of time a Savior will come. While doing his ordinary job at home, St. Simon would never forget, either in early morning or late evening, to visit the Temple where God dwelt, lest he might miss the Savior.

Like his death on the Cross when the sun hid in darkness and where many people were shouting on a shaken earth "Truly he is the son of God" as they were beating their breasts. Jesus said these are the signs of the end of the world… "Take heed that no one leads you astray…many will come in my name saying I am the Christ…nation will rise against nation…there will be famine and earthquakes…love will grow cold… those who survive all these will be saved." (Mathew 24:3-7; 12-13).

Satan, our tempter, did not also know when our Lord would be coming. When he saw Christ in Garandenese he immediately knew it was the Savior, and he asked…"What have you to do with us Jesus, Son of the most high God? Are you going to torment us <u>before our time</u>? (Mark 8:38).

Christ pointed to the swamp where one could see a herd of sheep nibbling on the grass up on the hill. Satan said they were part of a legion of 2,000 sheep which drowned in the swamp as they made their way into the dark bowel of the earth, (Mark 5:5-23). See, how destructive devils can be? Two thousand demons could stay in our system that could drive anyone crazy and behaving like the wild man in Garandenese, whom Jesus exorcised.

In this short dialogue, it is clear that Satan was afraid to know when the time Jesus will come to appear before him and his legion. Why afraid? Because the suffering of his followers will then be doubled.

While, on the other hand, when Jesus will appear, all Saints in Heaven will have their happiness and joy doubled. At this instance, there will actually be no tangible discrimination between Satan's followers and the Saints in Heaven because the amount of pain inflicted by the devils will equal to the amount of joys received by the Saints in Heaven.

At this point, there will be no more Purgatory or souls wandering in Limbo. One is either in Heaven or in Hell. Please be reminded that all people in Heaven are Saints. Those in Purgatory, can have their hopes doubled and they will be marching towards Heaven as Saints at the end of time.

Satan's story has a some of similarities with that of St. Simon who had been waiting for the coming of our Savior in the Temple. Of course, St. Simon never expected to see a child, much less, an infant visiting the Temple.

Perhaps, the Holy Spirit had kept Jesus' visit a big surprise for him. St. Simon's faith was much more than enough to eventually make him see our Lord perhaps either as a young man or even as an old man.

After many years of waiting St. Simon grew a lot older. His hair had become white, his beard grew long and he walked weary, lumbering in the late afternoon dusk, still faithfully going to the Temple. He was an old man.

In all these years, his faith never faltered. He knew his faith was not just on his own merit but more because of God's mercy and love. All he did was to cooperate with God's grace, not by reason but by faith alone.

When St. Simon saw a couple coming to the Temple, he felt something good was going to happen. He had seen many, many years, people or even just couples visiting the Temple mainly to pray. But he saw that this couple, approaching the Temple, appeared different ...surely his faith had shown deep in his heart that this scenario was different for it greatly uplifted his spirit.

Thus, as the couple was about to pass by St. Simon, he must have bowed his head and kept his arms open, appearing ready to receive the infant Jesus. Mary tenderly handed to him Baby Jesus. When St. Simon received Baby Jesus in his arms, he felt immensely happy as if Heaven had gone inside his heart.

To the amazement of St. Joseph and Mary he said, "This child is destined to the cause of falling and rising of many in Israel and a sign to be opposed by many (Luke 2:39)."

SYNOPSIS: St. Simon could not share what he did not understand about the beginning of his end...a journey to the world beyond. And so do I. The lessons I obtained from my life experiences, grounded on my faith, led me to believe that I am a thousand miles away from my understanding of the kind of life and place where I would spend my eternity.

Jesus reminds us, "I go to prepare a place for you." To this, Thomas responded..." How can we know the way?" Jesus answered, " I am the way, the truth and the life," (John 14: 4-7).

Therefore, I could say, that your life might be entirely different than mine. Yet, our goal is the same...to go to Heaven. Hence, sharing with each other our past experiences in life, might help us learn how to improve our own journey to Heaven.

Otherwise, it could be our journey to Hell. One of our greatest gift from God is the gift of FREE WILL, one which after death we can no longer enjoy and if improperly used on earth, will ensure our life in Hell as it would ensure a place in Heaven when following God's will in our life.

The argument of inherited weaknesses is no reason or excuse for doing what is sinful because our Free Will is over and above to defy them all, plus supplemented with a conscience we do not own. Hence, very basis to make us pleasing before God or that of the devil, the choice is ours.

*

A Song for My Dad

This song is a lamentation of my failure to follow my Dad's life as my natural model or guide, His honesty in life, had somehow greatly influenced my journey towards the beginning of my end.

"Whenever my 82 year old brain
Falters in prayer in-between my sleep,
It is a reflection of the unhurried hoof steps
Of a tired and aging donkey.

I know I have to look
For a small corner and weep,,,
Under a troubled Heaven
Upon my downcast fate,

And still there is hope for a flickering light
In the dark tunnel of my world:
For a self-centered creepy black wolf
'Who' is bellowing in the dark of night."

*

Dad, My Natural Guide

During the time of liberation after World War II when Dad was appointed by Gov. Cabahug as Argao's acting Mayor (former Mayor was allegedly killed for having been suspected as a Japanese collaborator), a group of high ranking officials from the Veterans Department came to our house.

They wanted to give my Dad the rank of "Captain" and this meant he would be receiving a life time pension (provided they would get a share). In his Honest, unassuming self, Dad said, "Sir, I have never served the army." In view of this simple honesty from my Dad, our family lost a great deal of the hoped-for benefits. My Dad was not afraid of the truth. He was afraid of telling lies.

He had to scratch his balding head for the last penny to send us 13 children from Primary Schools to Colleges and Universities single handedly, very often trying hard to make both ends meet. There were times when I saw Mom weeping for lack of food and money. I never heard Mom blaming him or complaining about him. But despite our poverty, Dad never succumbed to the temptation of dishonesty.

There was one time when our class examination was already scheduled and everyone was required to pay their tuition fees before they could take the exam. Dad had no money to pay for our tuition. So he went to see the Rector of Ateneo de Davao with a request to allow him to pay at a later date.

The Rector refused his request. Dad was forced to sell his machine, a generator that gave us light at home during the night. After losing the machine, we had no choice but to use candle for light, especially at night when we needed light most to study our lessons.

I don't know how he easily found a buyer for his machine, but he was able to pay our tuition on time. Like my brothers, I was able to take my exam on 4 subjects. However, while my other brothers passed all their subjects with flying colors, I failed in Mathematics. Dad probably never learned about my failure.

I wonder, if you were in my shoes would you tell your hard working Dad? Brod Lading got straight ones (highest) in almost all of his subjects. At the end of the semester he went up the stage to receive his honor card with people clapping. Did I clap? I did quietly. I only wished so hard that I too could have his brain.

There was a time when Dad thought he could succeed his father, Papa Anoy as Mayor of Argao. He actually ran for Mayor in 1937-38 against his cousin. But after the counting he was informed that he lost by 26 votes. There was a clamor for a recount and when this was done under proper supervision, the result was the exact reversal… Dad in fact won by 26 votes.

It was discovered that someone had manipulated the votes to make it appear that Dad lost. After his term in office and a new election was to be held he was offered again to run for Mayor. This time he declined and instead started a business of buying and selling copra, a career, he thought, was much more honest than politics.

An acid test of Dad's honesty especially in the way he ran his copra business was when one time he sold his copra at Tabacalera in Cebu City, (about 56 km. from Argao). Upon arriving home in Argao, he discovered that his customer, a Spaniard, actually paid him double the cost of his socks of copra. Immediately, he drove back for almost an hour to Cebu to return to his Customer the excess payment. He did this despite the fact that he urgently needed funds to move his business.

During the time of both his poverty and prosperity alike, Dad trusted God with all his mind and deep in his heart. Every morning he would spend hours, praying on his knees, and reading the Holy Bible that was why I noticed his knees were callous which unusually appeared black.

Callous, if you one, does not appear black. It might be that kneeling for hours before Christ's crucifix for decades perhaps without his awareness blood slowly sipped into his callous eventually turning his callous black. Shall we say, he had the wound of Christ behind this black callous? I don't know but it does seem to rule out my skepticism. He was a holy man in his life, no doubt.

During mealtime he would seldom say a word about God to us. It seemed as if he depended on our parish priest to do the teaching about God to us. However, largely because of his virtuous life, he became our model a shining example of how life should be properly lived.

*

Who Was Dad's Natural Guide?

It is very important that as a Father we live a good examples to our children. Just like my Dad, I think, he could not think of any natural model to guide his life than the life of his father, Mariano Abear, popularly called by the people in Argao as Papa Anoy. He was well known as the "Father of the people."

How did Papa Anoy earn the title, "Father of the people" in Argao since he was only an ordinary fisherman just like Christ's disciples? I can remember two vivid events out of the many simple deeds he made after arriving on the beach from a night of difficult fishing.

Normally, when he arrived on the shore after a night of fishing, people would meet him to buy his fish. But there were also those who did not have the money to pay, yet were there to meet him just the same. He recognized the familiar faces of the latter and knew their desire to have even just one fish. Knowing this situation, he would give them his own share of fish or the ones he was expected to bring home as food for his own family.

Upon arriving home Mama Ciana, his wife, would ask for the fish so she could cook them for the family's meal. Papa Anoy would just say …"Here is some money buy a canned Sardine in the market." Without any complaint (as most wives usually do) she would go to the market and buy.

The second incident happened along the beach, when he saw 3 men bullying an old man, teasing him saying he had "big eggs." Papa Anoy could not stand the scene. He told them to stop. Instead of obeying him, they positioned themselves for a fight.

Little did they know that Papa Anoy used to be a judo expert so he threw them one by one far into the sea. These two events (fish sharing and 3 bullies) plus a number of others spread like wild flower. All these earned him the title of "Father of the people."

When election time came for the first Mayor of Argao probably in the late 1850s, people urged Papa Anoy to run so that he can serve as the first town Mayor. He was not only the "Father of the people" he was also known as a person who did not know how to say "no." He was a "yes" man for anything good he could do for others.

But, he had two major problems: first, he had a Chinese family name "Tan" and second he did not possess high educational attainment. For the first, it was easy, they just changed "Tan" into "Abear." Second, his short informal education was simply replaced by his high faith in people and his positive attitude in life and to others.

He was running against a school Supervisor who would openly attack him, telling the people how could they vote for a "no read and no write" man. Papa Anoy would answer that the Supervisor was correct and they should vote for the Supervisor instead of him. When election was over Papa Anoy won by a land slide. The Supervisor left town.

After his term of office as the first Mayor of Argao, he went to Kansuji, a mountain, 18 km. away from the Argao town proper. He had to do this because he knew he would not be able to say "No." should the people ask him to run for another term. But mainly due to his lack of formal education, he chose to give others a chance to run the town.

When he had a stroke at age of 66 in Kansuji his last words to Mama Ciana was, "Pasayloa ako sa akong mga sala" (Forgive me for all my sins) and he peacefully passed away. When people heard about his death they stopped whatever they were doing and went to his home. He was carried on a Hammock by 8 people from Kansuji to Argao proper. People never saw before such a large crowd following his funeral march to the cemetery.

Should you have a chance to visit Argao, you will see "Mariano Abear Street" named in his honor. Unfortunately, a visit to the Municipal building will show that, while all the past Mayors have their photos, the first Mayor had only his name, "Mariano E. Abear"

*

The Up Bringing of Papa Anoy

Mom told us a story when Papa Anoy was a little boy he was made to live in a rich man's house in Argao. This rich man did not send him to school. Papa Anoy would just look at the window and saw kids happily going to school. How he wished he could go to school too. But this was denied to him and he could not help but weep alone in the kitchen especially at night when he slept with the dogs, Mom said.

There was a time that Papa Anoy was caught eating on the table with the rich man's kids. The man shouted at him. "You are a slave you should wait until we are finished eating." Papa Anoy would just go down from the table, sit in a corner and wait for them to finish eating so he could eat should there be any left-overs.

Later, the story continued that when the rich man's wife died he started gambling. Soon, he ran out of money, then he started to sell his wife's rare collections of statues: First, Mother Mary wearing a crown of gold and the rest of the collections followed such as St. Joseph, St. Michael and other precious items until everything was gone as he continued to lose in gambling. It was known that this rich man died in dire poverty.

*

Our Lady of Lourdes

The story of Papa Anoy, a "no read no write" man, reminded me of a Saint, similar to him, in life. She was a "no read and no write" Saint: St.Bernadette Sobirous of Lourdes, France.

When she declared to her parents and parish priest that she saw our Lady, all of them including her poor parents asked her to say it was not true. But she stood by what she said, even if she was threatened with imprisonment and even death.

Following the instructions of our Lady, she dug the ground with her own bare hands. Some people in the scene thought she was getting crazy. But it eventually produced a spring. With the water from the spring, it began to heal people of their illnesses. Very soon, Lourdes in France became known all over the world. People from different countries came to visit Lourdes in their desire to be healed of their illnesses.

Born on January 7, 1844. Bernadette lived the life of a nun and passed away on April 16, 1879. She was canonized as a Saint by Pope Pius XI on August 15, 1933.

My personal experience attests further to the miracles at Lourdes. I had a very severe back pain and I would lay in bed for weeks on end. We decided in 1978 to go for a pilgrimage to France where our Lady of Lourdes and the miraculous spring were located.

When we arrived at the place, there was already big crowd from different countries who participated in a procession. People were waving flags representing their respective countries. We took our place following the line for those who wished to take their bath at the spring.

When it was my turn, a very respectful man gave me a gown as I undressed myself. I laid down on a bathtub that was connected to the spring. I prayed for healing. After soaking for about 15 minutes, I got up and felt that I was completely healed of my bad back which to date had not recurred. At times, I might have joint pains, characteristic of most old people at my age but not my back.

*

St. Michael's Monastery

1ˢᵗ row, kneeling (left to right):
Sr. Ma. Isabel Montebon, Sr. Mary Felicity Narit, Sr. Mary Gerard Betco,
Sr. Mary mark Bunado, Sr. Ma. Gabriela Escarro, Sr. Mary Germaine Mariano,
Sr. Mary Stephen Tajale, Sr. Mary Julia Udtuhan

2ⁿᵈ row, standing (left to right):
Sr. Mary Felomina Villarta, Sr. Mary Bertilla Romaguerra, Sr. Janet Marie Cabago,
Fr. Rex Mananzan, SJ, Sr. Ma. Michaela Maravilla, Sr. Mary Cleofe Narit

3ʳᵈ row, standing (left to right):
Sr. Mary Kateri Capadngan, Sr. Mary Joseph Garciano, Sr. Mary Therese Cañada,
Sr. Bienvenida marie Magalso, Sr. mary Clare Gilbolingo, Sr. Mary Pius Facultad,
Sr. mary Siena Bracero, Sr. Mary Julia Udtuhan, Sr. Mary Lorenz Ruiz

St. Michael's Monastery

In deep gratitude for my bad back's complete healing, my wife and I built a Monastery in Argao, my home town in the province of Cebu, Philippines. I gave up all my saving plus my wife's help, leaving me only a small amount of my pension.

We donated the Monastery to the Society of Angel of Peace, founded by Msgr. Cris E. Garcia. After my donation I did not know that Msgr. Cris was in fact my Apo. We dedicated the building in memory of our only daughter, Rossana Abear Surujdeo who passed away at the age of 38 as a result of two doctors in Canada who wrongly treated her.

At the back of the Monastery, we erected a life size statue of our Lady of Lourdes. In front of her is the statue of St. Bernadette Sobirous, kneeling, holding a Rosary. In the grotto Sr. Mary Siena Bracero had placed a light that stayed lit day and night.

I invited Joe Alvar, a relative of mine living in New York City to visit the, St.Michael's Monastery. Together with 17 of his friends and relatives they stayed there for four nights. Sr. Mary Siena Bracero took good care of them during their stay. Before Joe left he donated a certain amount. I later learned that he left a lifetime commitment to the Monastery, praise the Lord!

This Monastery is named, St. Michael's Monastery in honor of Argao's patron Saint. By the way, the Monastery is open for Tourism. So, if you plan to go there one of these days simply email to me so that I could arrange your stay in the Monastery. Write to me at <e_abear@hotmail.com> Thank you.

*

The Omens

If you do not believe in Omens, I will understand because maybe nothing like it ever happened to you before.

The First Omen: while Brod Lading and Uncle Ascio were working in the fishpond near our beach resort I would hide behind our house (a little forested by coffee trees) and would pass my time away sleeping on a Hammock.

One time, when I woke up, I found underneath my Hammock about 7 feet long, a snake's shed-off scale probably left by a big snake, we call "Sawa" (python). I told my Dad about it and he said, "Elmer, you will have a bright future." …Shall I believe that a snake can be my guide towards a bright future?

Uncle Ascio laughed with incredulousness, because I was known in the family as a lazy vagabond. How could a vagabond have a bright future? The name calling did not upset me because it was true. I could not help the comfort of being lazy just lying on a Hammock during work time.

The Second Omen - happened many years later after the first Omen. I was newly married to Imelda and we were still on our honeymoon stage, spending our time in my Dad's farmhouse in Binugao, a barrio in Davao.

One morning, when we woke up we found a 7 foot snake's shed-off, possibly a shed by a Sawa which could have left our room earlier. I told Dad about this incident and again he said, "Elmer, you will have a bright future."

I asked Dad, what made you predict that? He answered that I happened to have the good snake of Moses against the bad snake of Jehovah (Numbers 21:1). When we left Binugao, we took a flight to Cebu while everything we had was sent by ship. This ship on her trip to Cebu sank bringing down with it everything we had.

Then, I heard my Sis Carmen say, "Naga baan sa Dios" (you are cursed by God) for leaving Papa and Mama alone in the farm. I did not get upset because what she said might be true before God. I began to doubt if the snake's shed-off scale could in fact, be the snake of Jehovah, indicating I would have a dark future instead of my Dad's prediction of a good one. The future was not my eyes to see.

*

The "Road Less Taken"

In my increasing years of age, I tried to walk on this road less taken. My experience on this "road less taken" is: you will meet all kinds of people. Take a tip - prefer a good man who thinks he is bad, rather than a proud man who thinks he is good.

Pope Benedict XVI suggested that you consider everything as mere falsehood (Spi salve). Why? Because you have to be very serious in choosing the best way to gain eternal salvation of your own soul after your temporary life is over on earth.

We need to be reminded that when we face God our friends will not be there with us to defend or protect us. Immediately after death, we face God alone. Therefore, while still alive, we have to get things right before it is too late and we are faced with "a might have been situation."

Hence, "Be not afraid" (365X Holy Scriptures) that you might fail on several occasions. Try not to make excuses but rather face your failures head on and ask God's grace to help you out so that you may do better in the next round of trials and tribulations.

Get allergic to saying, "Sorry, I was busy" a lame excuse acceptable only to the same specie of man. Begin to pray, "Give me another chance Lord and by your grace, I will make it possible."

Try the brave and courageous road, the narrow unheralded road. The payoff is good. The falsehood of pride that Pope Benedict XVI was talking about could perhaps become like St. Peter's rock, the whipping post of penance and amendment of past sins which could make your life holier.

Yet, conversion to walk on a "road less taken" did not come easy for me. The narrow path was very difficult that at times I felt giving up when the wide road was just across. My super ego was full of incapacitating pitfalls of all kinds in Satan's handbook.

If ever I was able to shed off some sins, new enticing ones with sexy appeal would easily come. I could not understand the holiness of my Dad and Mom, never mind my brothers, (except Brod Emelio and Alfredo and my Sr. Carmen), who were of lesser evils (if not, were living like 'Angels') than I was.

Thus, whatever vices came out per result of my life spending in vanity of vanities became items for sale. But no one had either the interest or the courage to take them. My vices, which most of the time took the form of many sexual pleasures, appeared more like rubrics with a thousand deceitful faces ready for a sick person to pick-up!

How can I become a better person, a "solid rock" like St. Peter where perhaps Christ could build a new man in "his own image and likeness?" I had no other option but become a priest like St. Augustine of Hippo, one time a womanizer.

Therefore, I would give up the world by serving God as a Jesuit priest. God did not call me to become a priest for I was not worthy. I called Him. Realizing that I was not an honor student like my classmate, Arsenio Jesena, Asandas Balchand, I was sure the Society of Jesus, a group of undisputed intellectuals, would reject me.

*

My Journey to Priesthood

To overcome poor qualifications to join the Jesuit Society, my strategy was first to humbly apply as a Jesuit brother whose life is spent, washing dishes, preparing breakfast, dinner and lunch for the Fathers and doing other menial jobs. Who knows, after spending sometime I might be upgraded to join as I said, to be among "the undisputed intellectuals."

Surprisingly, when I told Fr. Paul Finster, SJ., Rector of the Ateneo de Davao College, of my desire to join the Jesuit Society as a brother, I was immediately accepted. That weekend I took a 7-day sea-voyage from Davao to Manila. A Jesuit Brother met me upon my arrival and immediately brought me to the Sacred Heart seminary in Novaliches, Quezon City.

When I arrived, Fr. McCan, the Spiritual Director, was on hand. When I grasped his hand I could feel his own blood was running thru my veins as if I was lifted up from Hell to Heaven. I found out later that everybody had the same experience as I had. This man must be a living Saint.

One evening during our locution he told us a story: which was basically my own life's story which confirmed I was not called to become a priest. He was probably right. Although I tried, serving the good Fathers their breakfast, lunch and dinner, mopping the endless floor in sight, I could not stand it. It was not that I lacked the humility to become a Jesuit brother like brother, St. Rodriguez. It was not my vocation. Period. A month later, I left.

To challenge Fr. McCan's knowing my heart, I entered another seminary, San Jose Seminary in Quezon City. I was financially supported by the late Msgr. Clovis Thibault, PME. from Quebec, Canada, doing missionary work in Davao, Philippines in the 30's.

Yet, after a year I got so ill of TB I had to leave the seminary. I could not understand why I got TB when back home I survived on dried fish and maize. While in the Seminary we even had a difficult time to choose the food from so many varieties offered during mealtime. Jesuits believe that good food makes a healthy body and mind. But in my case, it worked the other way.

Anyway, since I was not healed after a year of treatment, Fr. Bazinet P.ME. came to our house and told Mom that priesthood was not my vocation. After he said that, I went into my room and wept. For the first time, I was shaking and went into convulsion (Nag kirig kirig intawon ko. Mom came and assured me that it was not the end of the world.

*

My Path to Study Medicine

Although hesitant, because my recent x–ray was still positive for TB after two years of treatment, I had no choice but to trust God and just try to enroll at Southwestern University (SWU), school of Medicine.

My brother, Dr. Johnnie, told me that if I would graduate from S.W.U. a low standard University, I would become a mang hihilot (a masseur). Brod Lading, my confidant, said, "Brod, you're too old to study medicine and besides Papa is broke."

For Dad to recover after Brod Johnnie finished medicine at the University of Santo Tomas, I landed a teaching job at St. Miguel's college in Padada, Davao. I experienced 2 incidents in Padada, Davao.

The first incident: there was a class that no teacher could handle. Sister Jane called me to handle this 3rd year, all boys class. True enough every time I wrote on the blackboard chalks would rain on the blackboard. As I turned around everybody looked like a Saint.

Finally, I caught one and I shouted at him to stand up and go home. He did. The next day he came with a revolver tucked in his belt, obvious enough for me to see. I thought I had to confront this guy or I would be a lame duck teacher.

I confronted him and told him to shoot me otherwise I said his revolver was plastic. I knew it was a real gun. He stood up. For a moment, everybody seemed to take a deep breath. I thought if he would shoot me, then I would be finished. He turned around and went home. For the entire the year I enjoyed teaching this class.

The second incident - was about a beautiful lady. She was my student in my evening class when I was teaching Philosophy and Drama. She seemed to have an eye on me. She appeared popular among the boys.

One evening my Landlady invited her to pass the night in her house. That particular night everybody went out to see a play downtown. We were left alone. My bed was right across her room, a room without a door.

Meanwhile, she was moaning and appeared restless in her bed. I knew what she wanted. Being human, I got a little bit fired up and was led into temptation to go to her room. But as I was near the window two peeping toms fell down into a pig's sty and I was delivered from this evil, Amen. I could have done sex with her since the two peeping toms were gone. I got clearance from Satan.

But instead, I went back on my bed, cooled like a cold red apple in the fridge. An hour later my Landlady with her children arrived and slowly climbed up the stairs. The lady across my room seemed to have mellowed down. So I had a good night sleep.

In the morning I learned that the two peeping toms were, in fact, my uncle and my Landlady's husband. I did not know I was being set up for good. I was not upset but silently thanked the two peeping toms who ironically saved me, from the 'pleasure' of sex.

To be fair with Satan, I thought of writing incidents where I was led into temptation and where often than not, he won. Especially during times of weakness, I usually violate either the 5th, or 6th or 7th commandments of God.

I had written the 5th (thou shalt not steal) and 7th (thou shall not tell lies) commandments of God in most of my true to life stories with no problem. My intention for writing was mainly to inform my readers that stealing and telling lies have bad consequences.

However, sorry for Satan but I could not write my failures in the 6th commandment (Thou shalt not commit adultery) but just a foible because of its pornographic nature. No one would benefit reading the work of Satan unless one is his friend. Satan has a lot of friends in his porno presentations in the internet.

Whenever I write and whatever I do, my intention is always to offer them for the greater glory of God and never for the glory of Satan. Nowadays, we see and hear a lot of Satan's successes especially when we listen to the six o'clock news where seldom the good work of God is mentioned. This is with the exception the EWTN, a Catholic global television network.

Satan has found his mouthpiece where the media from the left (mostly referred to as some Democrats in USA) would appear to twist the truth. For example, the news reported that the Muslims attacked the Cathedral in Cebu, Philippines but in fact it actually happened in Jolo, not in Cebu.

*

Life at South Western University

After three years, Dad was ready for me to start my ambition to become a Doctor. Dad told me to enroll at Southwestern University in 1967 because it was cheaper.

My problem was that my recent chest X-Ray's result still showed that I was still positive for TB, despite my long-term treatment. Anyway, I had to pray very hard and hoped, that by the grace of God, I would be able to overcome my impending bad luck, (in Visayan " dimalas").

At the Southwestern University all applicants were required to have an x-ray before admission. I got nervous. My x-ray was done and I hoped for the best. I was surprised! My x-ray showed no trace of TB at all.

Something made me feel that more than just my prayers, a heavenly blessing must have caused a miracle to happen. I had no idea whatsoever, what future would be for me. So, I said to myself, "Whatever will be, will be."

Having been a scholar as Editor-in-Chief at the Mindanao University where I obtained the degree of Bachelor of Science, major in General Science. It was not difficult for me to become the Literary Editor-in-Chief of "Quill" at South Western University.

During my third year medicine along with three scholars like Almagro and Buen, I was sent to Manila to compete with other seven medical schools during their school festival.

Since I was not a scholar in medicine but the literary Editor- in- Chief of the University's school organ they expected me to answer any question outside of medicine. During the contest we knocked out all 4 representatives from 6 medical schools. Only the contestants from the University of the Philippines were left standing to challenge us.

There was no question in medicine that U.P. and S.W.U. contestants could not answer. So to break the deadlock they decided to ask a question outside of medicine. My partners looked at me as if to signal it was my turn. My nerves were up.

Whoever got the answer first must reach for the buzzer. The question was: who was the hero depicted on a 20 peso bill? Poor me, I was only familiar of heroes depicted on 1 or 2 or 5 peso bills.

The contestants from the other side seemed to have given us enough time. My partners were anxiously looking at me for my answer. I could not imagine what to answer until the buzzer lighted up from the other side and the answer was: "Apolinario Mabini!" They got it right. We lost because of my ignorance. When we returned home it was not good news that we brought with us.

*

What Happened at Cebu Institute of Medicine?

For some academic controversies I transferred to another school, the Manila Central University (MCU). When Dr. Aurora Alcarez, my Aunt, knew I was going to transfer, she recommended me to the Dean of the Cebu Institute of Medicine who was her classmate at U.P. I was immediately accepted.

Under Editor-in-Chief Joe Leyson, I became the consultant Editor of the school organ named, Escolaplian. Eventually, in spite of great financial burden, I finished medicine. My poor Dad and Mom were eagerly preparing to fly to Cebu from Davao to attend my graduation.

Since I was a transferee from South Western University, it was not an honor for the school that I should march during the graduation. To justify such an idea I was grilled with so many questions during the round by doctors doing their Residencies while our consultant Dr. J. Poblete was with us.

One by one the Residents grilled me like steak to the finish until I committed a blunder which disqualified me to march with my fellow doctors for the upcoming graduation. They got what they wanted.

A week before graduation we all gathered for orientation at the conference hall to talk about the program. Since it was announced that I could not march with my fellow doctors during this meeting Dr. Espina stood up for me and threatened to protest.

Sensing that I was a disturbance, I stood up and spoke emotionally that I did not want to cause trouble for the upcoming graduation and would instead attend to see them graduate. One of my classmates perhaps touched by my speech became misty eyed. For a moment, there was deafening silence.

During graduation I was there, sitting in the Auditorium as I watched them marching to receive their diplomas. This night, I saw my girlfriend, Imelda, who graduated Cum Laude in Pre Med and was first ten in our class. Her parents, Domingo and Lucia were there with their big smiles, proud of her achievement.

A professor of internal medicine and my classmates knew I was there present to witness this once in a lifetime event. My classmates perhaps understood what I did understand by their pathetic glances at me as they passed by on their way to receive their diplomas.

You know, at that very moment, after 10 years of hard struggle I had a lingering taste of great disappointment. In other words, I was there just like their parents with their big smiles to share their happiest moment. The only difference was, I was their classmate who did not receive my diploma. That night, regret and humiliation, came over me in a big way.

All these humiliations made me realize the difference between me and the world. Thank God, I learned early enough to accept my impending demise and remembered what Jesus said when I was still in the seminary, "Learn of me, for I am meek and humble of heart" (Matthew 11:29).

The falsehood of life in the long run had made my life simpler and joyful. Indeed, the world will stand aside to a man who owns himself and accepting his weaknesses for the love of God. This is not to say that the world outside is a bad influence. In fact, it may be that the world could be better off without me.

*

Predestination

Before I reach the end to start, let me remind you the 15th promise to our Lady to St. Dominic which says, "A Rosary is a great sign of Predestination." To be basically in union with God's will I am humbly predestined to Heaven. Like any Catholics I must always be in the state of sanctifying grace. In short, we do not own ourselves as Christ said, "Die to yourself, come and follow me, "(John 20:33).

Indeed, I was not free the day that I tried to die to myself in order to follow the word of our Lord to become God's image and likeness (Gen. 1-27). To recall, God, out of his mercy, had kept me out of the seminary. God might have thought, a sinful man like me was not worthy to serve him as a priest.

I did not know what was in God's plan what predestation He had for me until I laid my eyes on Imelda. There was a woman while I was at S.W.U whom I had an affair. But she came and went without a dent in my heart but Imelda was different. Whenever I missed her I felt down, sad verses would come out from the deep recesses of my heart and I would sing this song:

I am a lonely seed,
Driven by a wild wind
Into a dry abandoned field,
Bare shire shoe no place to walk, eh!

I pray…
May the good Lord send
My dry roots rain,
A lot of rain,,,,

That in due time
I burst rose beauty on high
Be not a passerby
But a dream that might come true.

*

God's Providence

Whenever healthy loneliness strikes me, my heart and mind are set on God's providence. Could you imagine, for a few seconds, God's love which seemed to appear inside me became my only treasure? The only thing good inside me? My only hope to cling to?

Without God, sin in our soul is like a crab in a slow boiling water. Just as the crab did not know when he would turn red we would not know when we had died before God. Hence, whenever sin is denied, the market place of the mind is wide open for ownership and operation by Lucifer.

Although "the body is alive but if the soul is dead, the person is actually a walking dead among the living." Have you heard such a saying? May be some people did not know what they were doing, Jesus begged His Father from His cross, saying "Father, forgive them for they do not know what they are doing?"(Mathew 11:27; Luke 23:34).

*

A Lingering Light of Hope

For my wife to see amidst my own darkness she must be my light of hope that came down from Heaven. My board mate, Suckang told me, "You are fortunate to marry her because she is the most naïve lady I've ever known."

For fair and balance, I did not expect that from one of her closest friends, (whom Imelda often went out with on weekends for fun), whispered into my left ear, "You will be very unhappy to marry her." Anyway, not minding both opinions I wrote this verse before we got married:

Come Chosen Woman

Come chosen woman come
And sing for me
Lift up my heart
From fear by one wink
Of your unselfish recognition
And thou shall brighten my soul
To make me happy and unafraid.

Walk with me
In the green meadow
That holds communion in the fresh sun
Come, chosen woman, come
And sing for me
Be the song
That I only want to hear.

After several years of our marriage I noticed, her being naive was tantamount to the innocence of a child, untainted by the vanities of the world around. Her love was action while mine was often words. Diversity made our marriage unbreakable.

To confess to you: In my life time, I have met several women, but no one has ever perfectly fitted the hole in my heart, until I saw my lingering light of hope, Imelda, at the Cebu Institute of Medicine.

*

Then, Lucifer Came

At the zenith of my love with Imelda, when everything was fine, Lucifer came to break our marriage of true minds. One day Satan brought happiness to me when I saw a beautiful woman that, like, I was ready to lose everything that was spiritually built up within me after many years of praying and sacrifices.

She was very beautiful and attractive, married (whose husband was away) she looked 34x24x34 inches by waistline. There was indeed a clearance on the road towards her. I said to myself as I went down the stairs to see her, "I have to do this and accept to stay in Hell." The moment I sold myself to Satan, peace of mind and heart to do his will inspired my whole being.

As I opened the door on my way out to see this woman, I unfortunately saw my wife driving her car. I was surprised! It was Wednesday, normally she would come to visit me on the afternoon of Fridays after work at 5:00 PM. My plan had to be postponed perhaps for another day. Imelda and I went thru the normal motion of the usual weekend.

Sunday evening, she left for work, which was an hour and a half away from our home. I was very curious why she came Wednesday morning instead of her usual Friday evening. I called her and she emphatically said, "Why, are you asking such a question when you know very well, I always go there after work on Friday evening?"

That definitely shocked me, and I asked myself, "Who then accompanied and slept with me for almost 3 days?

I was shocked. Humbly, I came into a bitter realization, and I asked myself, "Can Imelda handle my flame, flare, crush with another woman? I don't think so. Had it happened the other way around, yes – but over my dead body."

I could not think of any, except of Mama Mary. For the first time I realized that our Mother in Heaven "loves me more than I love her" and that goes to all her children of the world.

I don't know about you, but my reaction was and still is painful to remember. Imagine, I abandoned Mama Mary (not to mention my Angelic wife) in favor of the opportunity offered to me Satan, my old buddy especially when I was young and foolish.

The fact is: I did not even pray to Mama Mary to avoid this offer by Satan. I was willing to go to Hell. But she delivered me from this temptation without my consent. How did it happen? I could not think of any except she cut off guard by sending an Angel in the appearance of my good wife, spending more than 2 days with me.

How could anyone think I was imagining? Why was I saved to deserve Mama Mary's concern anyway? In my modest way, for sure I never miss reciting the rosary daily which had saved me from several near-death experiences in the past.

With this event I was unaware for the first time that my faith with our Lady, reciting her Rosary daily since childhood, whether mumbling at times or heartfelt was credited to me. It had made me discover that my faith was like a tip of an iceberg. I was solid strong from a Satan cruise that went apart as it hit the tip of my iceberg. Our devotion and faith to our Lady play an important role in our salvation. It did to me.

Mind you, I did not pray to avoid this temptation, nor ask God to deliver me from this evil. For Mother Mary to save me where I was heading and sent an Angel that I did not ask truly reveals to me that indeed Mother Mary's love for us is more than the love I had for her or we have for her. Our unceasing devotion to her like reciting a Rosary daily pays us when we (unaware) need us most. As it was in my case.

To further emphasize the importance of reciting the Rosary daily, I remember one Christmas day in the late '50s this story. This is a true story. A plane was about to take up bound from Cebu to Davao. The plane was full of passengers on their way to spend Christmas in Davao.

In fact, at the door of the airplane was Modesto waving goodbye to his friend, Romeo, and laughing because he missed the plane. He could no longer be accommodated because the plane was standing full of passengers. Inside this this plane was Miss Tabora who I assumed was starting to pray her rosary as the plane started to taxi on her way up into the air.

Unfortunately, the airplane was not able to gain a higher altitude to overcome a small hill and hit a tree and burst into flame. No one survived except Miss Tabora, still strapped with her seat belt, a little far away from the scene, with her rosary dangling in her hand.

She was unscratched while she watched in horror the plane burning before her, consuming all the people inside. This incident made her left her comfortable life and entered the Monastery in Davao and became a monk. Did praying the Rosary save her from an untimely death?

In contrast, the parable of Jesus about a good Shepherd who left his 99 good sheep in the field and went out to look for that black sheep (after spending his inheritance) who was in despair to rescue him could be similar for Mama Mary to save me from adultery. I discovered her love when I asked my wife why she came Wednesday instead of Friday.

It reminded me also the third promise by our Lady to St. Dominic in 1640AD that a "Rosary is a protection against Satan." Jesus must have allowed an Angel disguised like my wife to spend days and sleep with me. For years, I could not figure out what God had in store for me for the future.

When I asked myself, "Why did God stop me for committing adultery for the first time out of my beautiful marriage?" You cannot think of losing a beautiful marriage in exchange for a moment of salacious pleasure. On top of that the reaction of the community where I served must be devastating.

Anyone who lives under the control of Satan knows the miserable consequences thereof. I know of my own confessor who lived for almost 30 years a saintly life serving our community, who when the police were on their way to arrest him for child abuse in a city far away some 3 decades ago, he panicked.

He did not probably know what he was doing, locked his garage and entered his car and died of carbon monoxide poisoning. NOTE: we cannot make judgment in this case and many others you know, as we remember what Christ said in Calvary, "Father, forgive them for they do not know what they are doing"(Luke 23:34).

In this event I mentioned above there was definitely the lack of forgiveness and compassion for him. It is sad that some of our religious leaders have joined the voice of the Media to defrocked and dehumanized Priests, Bishops, or Cardinal and to go out and do ministry no more (vocation, they love so much in their lives). We easily forgot what St. John Paul II's attitude who embraced a lost priest and told him to go back to his ministry and he did.

Have we forgotten what Jesus' attitude was when Pharisees and Scribes were holding stones to punish a woman caught in sin in front of him? Jesus looked at them and saw in their heart what kind of people they were and said, "Those who have not sinned cast the first stone" (John 8:7).

Silently, they dropped their stones and left. And to the woman Jesus said, "Your sin is forgiven, go and sin no more." I think today if we are faced with the same situation (I think we do) people, I doubt won't drop their stones: in some degree of paranoia. They want to see and witness the pain of sin how others suffer in public what they do in private.

Instead, we should say with forgiveness and compassion to every Priest, Bishops, Cardinal "Your sin is forgiven go and sin no more" (John 8:7) (which means by common sense they can continue their ministry if they want to). Jesus' statistic is very low compared to our present day situation, that is, 1 out of 12 was a traitor. Compared that today our statistic must be much lower, I guess, one out of a thousand disciples.

It might be worth mentioning here of a good priest who left his vocation. As a preview of this case, I remembered the day Mo. Angelica left her mother alone at home to follow His call to enter the Monastery. In a few months she broke her back when she slipped while doing a household cleaning in the Monastery.

This was followed by several surgeries on her back. On top of that, she got Asthma. With her wheelchairs and Asthma she, like a warrior, continued to speak about Jesus before the EWTN network, which she herself had founded. She suffered for decades until a healer from Italy, a woman was told by Christ to go and see Mo. Angelica and heal her back.

When she arrived at the EWTN she told Mo. Angelica what Jesus told her. As I saw Mo. Angelica, I had the impression that she was first skeptical but obeyed her instruction. Mo. Angelica stood behind her while she prayed. Mo. Angelica noticed a change in the alter and she noticed she seemed was talking to Jesus.

After her brief prayer she turned around and told Mo. Angelica to walk (without her wheelchair). Mo. Angelica knew she would fall flat on her face if she dared to. Somehow, she obeyed her to come forward. And as she did, she felt a healing of her back and the strength to walk. Mo. Angelica did not only walk but was dancing with joy.

She asked Fr. John Mary to dance with her. It seemed a symbol of a living Saint dancing with a human being, Fr. John Mary. I wished on my mind I was Fr. John Mary and helped me in my struggle, though rarely to be faithful with my wife. Well, thanks, at age 82, God I am still with my wife. At present, I do not understand why my wife loves me. Alleluia!

CAUTION: Any more than we cannot assume God's mercy we cannot undermine the power of Satan. That is, just as Jesus of today is present in the Blessed Sacrament, God the Father's sacrifice and ransom him for our salvation. Jesus said, you want to go Heaven take up my Cross and follow me for at the end there is everlasting joy.

And so is Barabbas of today, Satan's ransom for our eternal damnation. Satan must have said, "Take up your gold and follow me for at the end is my kingdom for you to enjoy eternal suffering and torment without end.

Very easy to identify Barabbas of today - mothers who kill their babies in their wombs, same-sex marriage, the private practice of homosexuals and lesbians, murderers, transgender that would make it easier to make sex at toilet room.

No doubt the devil has creeped further to destroy the morality of our nation; the list of Satan's 'honorees' cannot fill up this page. "Watch and pray that you may not enter into temptation," Christ reminded us (Matt 26:47; Galatians 5:17). Of course, judge not and you shall not be judged the immoralities of their lives that belong to God alone. Our role in salvation is only to pray and hope a better life for each one of them.

Mind you, whether my soul is in the state of sin or in the state of sanctifying grace I pray 50-100 rosaries daily. At the back of my sinful heart, I've faith Mama Mary is looking after me. So that it does not really matter with me if after death I go to Hell, Purgatory, or Heaven. What matter with me that as long as Mama Mary and Jesus are in my heart after death I would be in the right place where they are.

You know, Satan could still play my old record of immorality, which was a dead issue by God's mercy after my confession. But now if I take off my eyes from Jesus (as it happened in this case) like Peter who sank into the shark infested area because he took "count of the wind," (Matt 14:35) it could have happened to me. It almost did.

Suppose I ended up into the fire of Purgatory for a thousand years my confessor told me if my loved ones would pray for me, it would shorten my time. Do not forget that the intensity of fire between Hell and Purgatory is the same according to Mo. Angelica of the EWTN. The only difference souls in Hell do not have any hope to go Heaven while souls in Purgatory, yes, they are suffering with joy but with hope that one day they would be in Heaven.

I remembered what my mom said during my childhood years, she told me to kiss the hand of a priest and I would obtain 300 years indulgence. I asked Mom what she meant by 300 years indulgence, and she said the 300 years indulgence would shorten my stay in Purgatory. Nevertheless, I had stopped this practice for decades until I got old.

Recently, after Mass I started to restore kissing the hand of our Parish priest, Fr. J. Shurtleff, Fr. J. Thomas, and Fr. J. Morgan at the door of Notre Dame Church. My wife was greatly surprised since no one in New York would ever do this act.

Perhaps, she might have thought since I do not have many years to live due to my heart condition (the thought of my death would drive her crazy) it was a good thing to say goodbye to our parish priests in anticipation of any day I would go to the other side.

Whereas during my years of adulthood I used to whip my back with my belt after committing sin of the flesh but it did not help to lower my testosterone level, so I abandoned it. Now at age 82 I whip my back every Tuesday and Friday with my belt for sin committed against the Holy Spirit in repentance for my sin and others. These are graces probably I earn thru no merit of my own.

*

Reflection
of My Padre Pio's Visit

When I and Imelda entered the Church of Padre Pio in Pietrelcina there were many flowers, but I saw no roses. However, I smelled the scent of roses and so did a few other people, but Imelda did not. She might not know but her faith was sufficient. While as for me, I needed it to increase my faith.

When we entered Padre Pio's room which was a part of the Church, the lively Monk in charged allowed us to touch Padre Pio's gloves. His gloves were made of white cloth and were drenched with dried blood hung on the wall. Padre Pio's blood was caused by Satan's whipping, which I thought Satan would have not stopped doing until Padre Pio surrender his soul to him. But I supposed Satan got tired and he instead returned back to Hell and to just try again on another day. Satan, I think, never gives up on someone who is trying to live a holy life.

Every Friday, back home in New York, I whipped myself with my belt in atonement of the scars of my sins (left after I received forgiveness in confession before Christ in persona Christi). It was not a hard whipping with my belt, but just a pain enough that poor me can handle.I asked God why not allow Satan to whip me.Perhaps, I got the answer from Satan, that is I am not holy enough like Padre Pio. I think Satan is right. Pray for me my Guardian Angel Joel that I might become holy enough to qualify for Satan.

Anyway, I increase my flagellation almost daily when my wife is at work. Because if she would know, I think, like other people seeing me kissing the hand of a priest would think that I have gone nuts. The only person who would believe me is someone who I have something in common with, that is my SOE who thinks that I am "Wired with God." I hope the wire is not live because I am not worthy for a live wire. Unlike the fire that engulfed Francisco which did not burn him because he was holy, I might end up getting burned and experience Hell, instead.

*

If your soul has built up graces which make you holier in life due to your obedience of Christ's two greatest commandments, obtained thru prayers, sacrifices and confession they are all downloaded from your soul by one mortal sin.

But don't worry, the late Fr. Forbes Monaghan, SJ., Phd. told us in our class in Apologetics that those graces we lost by one mortal sin are loaded back into your soul by going to confession. One thing good with Christ he does not remember our sin after confession. We do it for a simple reason that remorseful, we promise not to offend Jesus again.

*

The Benefit of Confession

Every Sunday during my teenage life I never lost sight of the fact that every Sunday, rain or shine, I should receive Holy Communion. I knew I could not receive Holy Communion when I am in the state of mortal sin. I have to go to confession to get back my sanctifying grace which I often lost during my younger days the week before Sunday.

Therefore, going to confession before Sunday became an act of love for Jesus from me. This habitual sin of the flesh had even reached a point when the priest asked me, "Are you not tired doing that sin, again and again?" I felt so ashamed that I found it hard to answer him.

At the end of my confession and after having given me my penance before he closed the door (when I thought, he would not be Christ in persona but a human being like me) he said, "Pray for me."

That greatly astounded me, knowing I was forgiven by Christ through him. I could now pray for him since I was already in a state of sanctifying grace. It was so hard for me to believe that I, merely one of the "poor banished children of Eve," should be asked to pray for Christ's persona.

Many of my peers did not believe in confession. They would rather confess direct to God than to another human being. Ironically, I saw some of them receiving Holy Communion which explained to me why the line at confession was short compared to the much longer line receiving Holy Communion every Sunday.

Then I remembered what Christ said from the Cross, "Father forgive them for they know not what they do," (Mathew 26-27). It seemed they are spiritually better than me because I am not covered by what Christ said from the Cross. I know what I was doing was wrong. Hence, they could spend less in prayers than I do. Sometime, I wish I am like them not knowing what I do hurt our Lord.

Our Lady of Fatima

(Photo Credit: https://www.amazon.com/ Fatima-Painted-Religious-Figurine-Portugal/dp/B01NGYRESE

The Story of Our Lady's Golden Crown of Fatima

For the miracle that I was delivered from evil, I thought in gratitude for my protecting me I planned to replace the tinsel crown of our Lady of Fatima in my chapel room, a statue given to me by my niece, Aida with a golden crown.

By the way, what did our Lady of Fatima said to St. Dominic in 1613 AD in bologna, Italy when she appeared to him? She made 15 promises to St. Dominic that those who pray the Rosary daily would be protected, her 4th promise was, "A Rosary is a weapon against Hell (Satan) (St. Gema.com,2005)." And so I think I was.

I dreamt of decorating the crown of gold with colored gemstones all around. Each color would symbolize some significant events in the life of Christ which should be remembered as one takes the journey to Heaven.

Thus, Ruby is red, a reminder of Christ's blood as He pitifully hangs on the cross and yet still asking his Father for forgiveness for those who have done wronged Him. Emerald, a green color that symbolizes our Father almighty as the Creator of Heaven and earth. Diamond, a brilliantly sparkling white to signify the Holy Spirit guiding us on the narrow path to salvation. Finally, Sapphire, blue color associated with our Lady of Fatima who intercedes for us and who will be our guide as we enter the gate of Heaven.

At the Jewelry store in Watertown, New York, I showed to two lovely ladies, the simple tinsel crown. I inquired from them if they can make a replica of the crown, this time in at least 18 carat gold decorated with gemstones. They got so enthusiastic by the idea of making such a unique creation and after some calculations they showed me a purchase order amounting to $3,014.56.

For such a job, the amount appeared too expensive for my financial capability, an ordinary pensioner. But then, I said to myself…"Who cares about the cost! Nothing is too expensive if it is to be offered for our dear Mother in Heaven!" So, I signed the purchase order, presented to me, no questions asked. I even forgot to inquire when I would expect the work completed.

I thought two weeks was long enough. So I decided to return to the shop and was greatly disappointed when I was told that the man who was supposed to do the job, not an employee of the jewelry store, could not be contacted. However, they said they had already engaged him to do the re-designing of the tinsel crown.

To make sure I had enough funds to pay for the job-order, I returned to Ogdensburg, New York and went directly to my bank. There I ordered a Manager's check made out for the amount in the P.O. It took away a lot of my savings. I did not tell my wife about this expense mainly because I wanted to surprise her. Besides, I knew that anything for the Blessed Mother was always alright with her.

The following weekend I went again to Watertown. I showed them a receipt for the check I had prepared to cover the P.O. In fact, I left with them the receipt. I told them beforehand that only when the gold crown was already in my hand, would I give them the Manager's check.

After another 3 weeks, I was almost certain that the job would be completed. So, I returned to Watertown to pick-up the gold crown and give them the Manager's check. I approached the two ladies, but before I could even open my mouth, they told me the bad news.

They said that the man, who was supposed to do the job, was very upset because he was told by the bank, where he went to cash the "check," that it was "fake." It was beyond my belief that these two ladies and the man who would do the job did not know that it was just a receipt and not a "check." My goodness, I said to myself, and said to them…Good bye, thank you." Showing with my facial expression and body language how extremely exasperated I was.

Forgetting my 'surprise' plan, as usual, I had to share my disappointment with my wife. Soon after and without my knowledge she had immediately called the Bank to cancel the check. She told me it would be better if we had the gold crown done in Cebu, Philippines. It could be a lot cheaper, with perhaps better design execution and completed at a much shorter time

We decided to order in Cebu, the crown of gold decorated with gemstones. My wife was right! Although to be done at home by a man who owned a small jewelry shop, still he assured us that he would use as base material almost pure gold (22karats) and real gemstones.

For the complete work, he only charged us, $1,200.00. Bebot, my niece who lives in Cebu, promised to send me the completed work via a 24-hour service mail. However, the maker of the crown suggested not to have the item sent by air lest it might be damaged.

In my disappointment, I wrote to Bebot, to tell the crown maker that he had no business getting involved with the handling of his finished work. I have paid for the crown and it is mine to handle the way I want to.

Later, I realized my arrogance, born out of exasperation to immediately get hold of my crown and I sincerely regretted my action. I wrote a letter of apology to the crown-maker and hoped he would accept it.

There has to be a faster way for the Gold Crown to reach me in New York. I was already very eager to have it in y possession. We had no plan to go to Cebu again since we had just returned to New York after attending the burial of my wife's sister, Conchita.

With all my multiple physical disabilities, travelling long distances was not exactly palatable to my taste. Imagine, I was once a strong, heavy muscled man but now at age 82, I look very old, frail and visibly disabled. In the airport, I am even forced to use the wheelchair, pushed by a young lady, moving from one gate to another. Oh my, my current physical condition is indeed very humiliating!!!

But then again, fate intervened! Almost two months after the aborted crown delivery to me, we received a bad news from my son Butch that Patricio, my wife's brother passed away at the age of 83. Despite all the foreseen difficulties, we packed our things and left for the Philippines in a hurry.

After two weeks of prayer and vigil, Patricio was buried as we continued to hope and pray that he would be on his way to Heaven. We knew, that unlike me, my brother-in-law was a holy man. Were it not for the sudden death of Patricio, the gold crown could have gone via 24 hour air-trip to Ogdensburg, NY.

Instead, I had the privilege to carry the Gold Crown of our Lady in my arms back to Ogdensburg, NY. Upon arrival I gave the crown to my wife. I could not rule out the possibility that our Lady knew beforehand all the events connected with the gold crown.

My wife came into my small chapel and tenderly installed the crown of gold on our Lady of Fatima's head. Alone, from where I was sitting, the crown of gold with precious stones of red, green, white and blue were brilliantly gleaming in the sunlight. It was a magnificent and awesome sight.

I started to pray the four mysteries of the Holy Rosary, asking Mama Mary that she might be consoled by priests, nuns, and lay persons who have given-up their devotion to her. I also prayed that when I would die, unworthy though I am I should die while protecting her as our Immaculate Conception for the greater glory of the Father, Son and the Holy Spirit.

I started praying the Glorious Mystery before her. This was followed by reciting the Joyful Mystery. It was on the 3rd joyful mystery when Jesus was born in Bethlehem, that I suddenly sniffed a sweet odor I had never smelled before. It came and then went after I finished the joyful mystery.

When I started the sorrowful mystery, it seemed that the sweet odor was no longer just a whiff because it lasted longer to perhaps remove my Thomasian any doubt on my part. I fell on my knees as I continued to recite the sorrowful mystery and then followed by the luminous mystery by St. John Paul II. Then after completing the Rosary, I checked again my clogged-up nose to know if the sweet odor was still there, but it did not linger on.

To further my commitment to our Lady that I might find complete remission of my sin, committed when I sold my soul to Satan, I promised to honor our Lady her appearance in Fatima to pray every day 13 Rosaries either on my knees, frustrate or on my couch before her statue. I started last Jan. 30, 2019 hopefully until I die.

I think it would please our Lady of Fatima if we mentioned why she is called our Lady of Fatima. According to the Shia Muslim Fatima was the only daughter of Prophet Mohammed who was baptized Catholic before she got married to Congulo Herminez in 615 AD. NOTE: "While Muslims do not hold the same beliefs about the Virgin Mary they have a high regard."

At this time the war in the Middle East is actually between Muslim against Muslim from different factions. Christians are killed apparently to agitate the Vatican and were executed. I saw them on TV dressed in pink lining up for beheading. Hopefully, the title of Mary as our Lady of Fatima, though it may sound a long shot, might find its way to appease Catholics and Muslims alike in the near future.

*

I prayed for decades that like, Padre Pio, I would have the wounds of Christ too. But not like the kind of wounds espoused by Padre Pio. I just want the feeling of pain as the nail was driven thru my hand, the hand that committed the sin of the flesh, the heart that betrayed Jesus, and the feet that took the wide road of Satan.

Last December 25, 2018, Philippines time, between 2-3 AM I was wide awake and I felt a terrible pain I had never experienced before, as if a nail was driven thru my left hand three times and slowly faded away. Christ's Christmas gift for me? I wonder.

I assure you - no preconditioning of my mind nor dreaming. I was fully awake getting ready to recite (my routine) the hour of Divine Mercy at 3 AM. I thanked Jesus for at least I had experienced his pain.

Last February 17, 2019 (Feb 16, 2005) Rossana reminded me it was Sunday she entered the hospital and died 7 days after per my advise because she had flu for almost 2 weeks with fever at 40 and vomiting. How did she remind me?

My wedding ring which was suck on my left finger for decades and could not be removed without the use of soap and water came off from my finger without my awareness on that fateful day in the Hospital where she said to her companion, "Where is Dad and Mom?" I was surprised Imelda handed it to me. I forcefully put it back on my left finger and told her that there was no way my wedding ring could be removed without using soap and water.

She could not believe so she tried to remove my wedding ring and she could not. I do not know what she thought. I dare not ask her. It appeared to me that Rossana might have removed it to perhaps remind me to pray for her. I used to pray for her, on and off. So this time I promised to her, one rosary for her alone everyday till I die. So help me God!

Papa Anoy's apparition seen by Nong Doro and Nong Pastor

A State of Limbo

D o you believe in Ghosts? Believe it or not, Christ's 12 Disciples especially Thomas actually believed in Ghosts. Their belief was confirmed when they were in their upper room they saw Christ pass thru the locked door. They were amazed to see Christ's ghost.

When Jesus asked Thomas, the most doubtful among the 12 Apostles, to touch him, Thomas got bewildered. Would he dare touch Jesus, a Ghost? But then, "doubting" Thomas came forward towards Jesus and soon he touched His hands, he knelt down and cried, "My Lord and my God" (Mark 16: 1-20). This exhortation by Thomas has run down to our current century as we pray and affirm our faith especially when we eat his body and drink his blood in Holy Communion.

On this occasion, Jesus knew the rest of the Disciples were uncertain about what they had witnessed. Since Ghosts do not have a body to touch or eat solid food, Jesus asked them to give Him food,

Their eyes opened wide, as they watched Him eat. This was not the first time they heard that Jesus had risen. In fact, Mary Magdalene had already told them that she saw Him and she said "Yes, Jesus has risen." But the Disciples merely dismissed this as one of the usual .."You know, women's gossip."

In the Gospel, Jesus expounded on the idea of Ghosts in the minds of His Disciples. Jesus said simply that he did not come to save Ghosts or even to save good people but He came to save sinners. So, do I believe in Ghosts? Of course, I do.

Although Satan could also appear as a Ghost it does not necessarily mean that he is a Ghost. Although some of us (me no exception) sometimes feel the devil is inside us, this does not make us Ghosts.

Anyway, were it not for this weapon (the act of confession) instituted by Christ against the Devil, given to the priest in persona Christi (Luke 23:34), my soul like many others would perhaps be spending my after life in limbo, (in a way like Purgatory), drifting in different forms and scary figures in the abys between light and darkness.

Are there souls drifting between light and darkness? Definitely yes! Call it superstition but I don't because I have seen and heard so many evidences of this situation. To mention few scenarios, out of many I know from some very reliable and truthful people, who would gain nothing by telling lies...here are the stories:

(A). The Kapre (Ghost): One night in Argao, my Dad and two of his buddies, Aballe and Alcazarin (who later became the Sec. of Foreign Affairs under the Presidency of Carlos P. Garcia, from Bohol a small province of the Philippines) routinely at 4 AM were on their way to harvest crabs caught in their overnight traps. There was full moon.

They were surprised to find that the crabs had not come out. So they decided to pass their time at the maternity house nearby. While they were talking, all of them saw a large shadow creep towards them from behind.

As they slowly turned their heads they saw a Kapre (Ghost) standing, half naked, black, hairy 12 feet high, near San Miguel's Church, laughing at them. Each one of them ran away without even passing through trodden roads but on whatever space was available for their feet to bring them directly to their respective homes. At home, they heard the bell at San Miguel church ring... it was one o'clock past mid night.

On the late morning of the following day, they came back to harvest the crabs which they needed to sell at the local market. But they saw that the traps were scattered all over the place... all empty! This spelled the end of their business for the day... thet had nothing to sell!

(B). The Dwarfs: A group of people in their senior years were on their way at 3:30 AM to attend Mass at San Miguel Church. Suddenly, they were frantically knocking at our house!

My Dad opened the door and they asked for help because a group of dwarfs were chasing them. Dad picked-up a piece of wood and chased the dwarfs back to the marketplace. The dwarfs were seen going inside a canal and then suddenly disappeared. Where did they come from?

(C).The Scary Kapre: During World War II, the Japanese soldiers who occupied the schools as their garrison, saw during a full moon, a giant Kapre, smoking while sitting on the branch of the Acacia tree in front of the school. The soldiers evacuated the schools and never came back. The local Guerrilla unit headed by my uncle, Pastor Abear, was spared of the job of having to shoo away the enemy.

(D). Multo (Ghost) or Kalag (Soul) : uncle Pastor and uncle Doro were brothers of my father. Very often they would be at odds with each other as their tempers continue to rise. Back in Cansuji during World War II when Papa Anoy was still alive, he could easily resolve their heated encounters.

However, after Papa Anoy was gone, no one else could resolve their problem as they continued to fight each other. It appeared that there was bad blood between them. They could not settle their differences peacefully, so one day, they decided to shoot each other out, as in a duel somewhere near the mountains.

In Kansuji, there were two mountains and between them was a wide rice field. Uncle Doro and Uncle Pastor positioned themselves facing each other near the center of the rice field in-between the two mountains.

When they were about ready to shoot each other they suddenly saw Papa Anoy walking across the rice field. They were both aghast...then and there they decided to stop their duel. Both resolved that from then on they would settle their differences peacefully.

Some people called this apparition as the "ghost" of Papa Anoy (or "multo" in Tagalog). Still others call this in Visayan dialect as "Kalag"(meaning soul) of Papa Anoy. The question now is...do souls really return to earth? If so, why or for what reason?

It may be recalled in our basic Catechism that souls in Purgatory can pray for their love ones on earth. Of course, they cannot pray for their loved ones unless they know what is actually happening in their respective home and family. Thus, in some rare occasions God allows them to come down to earth to deliver a message.

This could probably explain why Papa Anoy appeared to the brothers who were about to duel. Papa Anoy's message was clear: "Papa Anoy, known as the "Father of Argao" did not want this beautiful valley where he grew up and died to be smeared with the blood of his own two sons." Note: that most appearances of ghosts carry with them simple messages which can be clearly understood by those who saw them.

Therefore, Catholics who do not believe in the forgiveness of sin thru confession might become a "Limbo" of their own making. It appears to me that "Limbo" can be interpreted as part of Purgatory just as Protestantism could be a part of Catholicism and Muslim part of Hinduism according to Neil Surujdeo, a holy and faithful Hindu who was the husband of my late daughter, Rossana.

*

Perhaps the Reason I Live Longer

I am now 82 years old, an age much older than my father and any of my 12 of my brothers who passed away. What could be God's reason for having given me a longer life? I think, my 12 brothers must have prayed so hard to God to spare me from falling into the hands of Satan because there is no night that I do not pray for them to enter the gate of Heaven.

Suppose this miracle did not happen to me, first I could not imagine the kind of life I would be forced to live under Satan's guidance. God alone, to whom I always put my trust, knew this in advance. Second, my brothers in Purgatory (assuming they are in Purgatory) won't be happy. They have to contend staying in Purgatory for a longer time.

Before I end this book, allow me to give you the lighter side of my life with my wife and 3 pets. For the last 23 years, we lived in this beautiful of Ogdensburg, NY where people are helpful, kind and gracious.

*

Of Dogs and Ground Hog

To ensure that I could have someone to talk with while my wife, Imelda was still at work at the St. Laurence Psychiatric Hospital, as a medical Pediatrician, she bought me "Potchie", a coton de tulear by breed, "Happy", a Shih Tzu, daughter of "Sandy."

Yes, I could talk to each of them when I was all alone with them. They knew their names and responds to me whenever I called them to my room. I could sense they expected to receive goodies from me everytime they come to me.

Each of them had a different characteristic. For example, "Potchie" must have thought that everybody was his friend and therefore, he assumed that their houses were also his. One evening, while I was in the kitchen, he turned loose from his leash, without me knowing what had transpired.

When Imelda arrived home from work she asked for "Potchie". I said he is just outside the house. She went outside to look for him and soon after returned inside the house and said "Potchie is not there." I went out to check the back of the house where his leash was tied and found the leash but without "Potchie".

Imelda got frantic. We both immediately went out and walked in opposite directions, in an effort to trace Potsie. Imelda went South and I went North passing through the green grounds on which we normally walk-on during Summer time.

I was already running all over the place, forgetting the pain of my arthritis and even my heart condition. I could not find him. An hour later, Imelda came to me and said "Potchie" was already back home.

Our dog "Potchie" in the arms of our neighbor and Imelda saying "… that's my dog!"

When the lady opened the door "Potchie" eagerly jumped into her arms, perhaps expecting to be hugged. Imelda saw this scene from the roadside. She approached the lady and said, "So sorry, he is our dog." The kind lady came over with a big smile and handed "Potchie" to Imelda.

Of the three dogs, "Sandy" was the only one who, when given her food, would first look at the food and raise her head up to Heaven as if to pray to God. The other two, Potchie and Happy would just rush to eat their food without even pausing to know where the food came from and much less to thank God for the food they were about to partake.

Happy was the most intelligent of the three dogs. Whenever she sees that I gave her less attention because I held only "Potchie" and Happy in my arms, she would look at me in disgust and then hide under the table. At other times, when she felt so depressed, she would go into seizures. A hug would resolve her problem right away.

Potchie

Sandy & Happy

Groundhog
(Photo Credit: https://youtu.be/9496GHahfh4)

On Ground Hog

To sum up my life at age 83 it is similar but not the same as a Ground Hog. A Ground Hog enjoys the rhythm of Spring, Summer and Autumn. He hides during Winter underground within the two walls of his room to sleep and fast all Winter long. At the break of Spring, he wakes up and comes out of hiding. I do not know if, like me, he also prays.

Every morning especially during early Spring I see Ground Hogs at the back of my house happily wandering around, eating and playing. We could also see them chasing for love their opposite sex, as if to regain their first Spring which Eve had lost.

The Ground Hog's humble life fascinated me because, as a disabled senior, my life is almost the same as theirs, confined essentially within the four walls of my room, not fasting like ground hogs but doing what normally a disabled person can still do. The following lines are verses, an insight that I was inspired to write about a Ground Hog, in relationship with myself.

*

I am a Ground Hog

When my Autumn's life is over, I go gentle into that good Winter's night under the ground. I am a Ground Hog in sinful condition, sin of the flesh, remorseful, fasting for 3 months till the break of cherry blossoms do I feel the spring tide showering into my soul.

Do I feel good as I am dancing with the Angel's rhythm? (I thought, it was my 2nd Spring). Little did I know, I am dead naked from the unholy ground.

It is in fact the blessing of my eternal first Spring, "hallowed be thy name thy kingdom come, thy will be done on earth as it is now I am in Heaven." Oh, Lord!

In the next verse below you will see how I spent my life in detail with my loving wife. I consider her my guardian Angel. She is kept within my heart, confined and attuned with a harmonious, sweet and bitter song such as the following:

My Angel in Human Form

Whenever I try to wash the dishes
Whereas before she would get upset
Because it was not done perfectly.
Now she would do it again
Understanding my disability.

Whenever I misplace my wallet
She would find it, add some dollars
In case I might trip a glass in the Mall
So, she won't have to bail me out
At the police station.

Whenever I forget where
My hearing aid is
She knows because I keep
Saying "yes" safer than
Instead of saying "No."

Whenever she forgets her bag
Outside of the door I pick it up
Steals a rare $10.00 bill for a drink
For what Adam lost, my first Spring.

*

WHAT READERS SAY

Elmer's MEMOIR pieces reveal a *KATOLIKONG SERRADO*. His are a sensitive conscience & a sharp mind formed by his parents, honed by his siblings and by people he met in life, & refined by his Catholic education in Jesuit institutions.

He completed high school at the Ateneo de Davao. He discerned in the Jesuit Novitiate in Novaliches that his temperament did not suit him to be a Brother. His health cut short his studies at San Jose Seminary - QC. Becoming a Brother or a priest was not his vocation, he realized early on.

Despite these seeming setbacks, he remained Catholic and stuck to the Church's values and teachings such as on abortion, the sacraments, life after death, temptation vs. sin, salvation, confession, Mother Mary, etc.

Worth citing is that youths of his times underwent corporal punishment, which lingered from Spanish era & applied on him at times by his father and exercised even by the Jesuits in Elmer's schools. Jug, posts, and whacking, & other physical castigation he experienced like other "naughty" boys.

These, ironically but fortunately, made him a disciplined young man and a tougher adult. God called him to be a doctor - a profession as noble as a priest's or a Brother's. While in medical studies, he met the love of his life - his wife Imelda, who has been his rock since then.

As a doctor, with his wife (a physician herself) ever by his side, he spent most of his professional life & retirement years abroad. Lately, because of age-related waning senses, he uses his time to write religious apologetics and, understandably, his memoirs. Books he has authored will preserve his memory among his loved ones. His visual & audio faculties, & his physical strength may decline somewhat - but not his mental and spiritual abilities.

By his Catholic faith, Elmer strives to be a man for others. He assists relatives in their spiritual, emotional & financial needs. Instead of enjoying his retirement savings all to himself & his family, he sponsors the Sisters of the Angel of Peace (SAP) in Argao, Cebu - his *yutang natawhan* (birthplace). This sponsorship is in memory of their daughter, Rossana. Only later, does he realize that the SAP is founded by his grandson, a Monsignor. As SAP's main benefactor, he is assured of the steady prayers for him by these wonderful nuns.

What a man to leave a legacy of tested, virtuous living, family love, steadfast character, service to others, & enlightened faithfulness to the one true Church!

May Elmer's life be crowned with the glory he so deserves.

Jose (Joe) Ortiza Alvar Jr.
Co-Atenean & longtime friend.

I have known Dr. Elmer Abear for many years and have always known him to be a man of deep conviction. His honesty and desire to always do what is right are truly on display in his latest literary effort.

Gerald Smith
PGK PSD
Knights of Columbus
Newfoundland, Canada

*

"Poignant and humorous, Elmer Abear's book could very well be a time travel journal. He brings you through a journey centuries back narrating his dependency from Spanish friars during the Spanish colonization of the Philippines down to his life in his birthplace in Argao, Cebu.

The book chronicles his youth, his time as a medical student, his life as a family man. He is a vivid storyteller: spicing his unforgettable sentimental stories with sprinkles of naughtiness and wit. He oftentimes depicts himself as a religious man with a human heart.

His foibles and impish experiences make you relate to your own life as an insecure young adult. He weaves in parallelisms of Catholic teachings in his anecdotes which are presented in a light and funny way.

Proud of his ancestry, he talks of his parents with great admiration and though he grew up in poverty, he speaks of it as if it were a privilege. If you want light reading with a touch of naughtiness, profound yet sincere narratives of a poor young man in prewar Philippines, this is the book for you. It will leave you with a smile after every chapter!"

Mary Ann Kuik
Business Lounge Staff
Schiphol Airport
Amsterdam, The Netherlands
Amsterdam, The Netherlands

ILLUSTRATORS

Mr. Joel M. Gatchalian, is the illustrator of this book. He studied at the College of Fine Arts, University of the Philippines. Worked at Quality Partners Company Ltd, a family owned business. Worked full-time with Pycon International as a member of their Marketing Staff. Worked as a gun-designer at Armscor Philippines. Owns a business in gun-designing and manufacturing. Joel is the co-owner and principal designer of Airpower Engineering Company.

***

Alton (15 yo) & Alette (10 yo) Abear. The siblings are the book cover designers. Both aspire to become graphic artists someday. According to them, the book, I Confess to You, contains their Great grandpa's stories of hardships and joys in finding God in his life. The interpretation of the book cover: The rays of the sun symbolize God's love and mercy. By staying under the sunlight, we receive God's never-ending kindness and provision. We can remain in the light by staying faithful to God's word and trusting in his will. Just like the Ground Hog and the Dog, whose gaze are focused on the light (Jesus), they are blessed with hope and love in their lives. No amount of problems, misfortune, and darkness around us can defeat and replace Jesus' promise of salvation. Only him can fill our lives with bright days, give us green meadows, and ultimately, a glorious, new beginning, . . . a Second Spring.

ABOUT THE AUTHOR

Elmer M. Abear, M.D, studied Priesthood in a Jesuit Seminary, San Jose Seminary, Philippines in 1978; Consultant Editor, Escolapion, Cebu Institute of Medicine in 1970; Literary Editor-in-chief, Southwestern University's school organ in 1966; Editor in Chief, *Mindanao Collegian,* Mindanao University, Graduated A.B. in 1969; English Professor, St. Michael's College, Philippines; 3rd Degree Member of Knights of Columbus. Author of 5 books. Married to Dr. Imelda Ramirez in 1972 and has 3 children: Rosanna, Butch, and Dave.

The End

Printed in the United States
by Baker & Taylor Publisher Services